Race for Relevance

5 Radical Changes for Associations

HARRISON COERVER AND MARY BYERS, CAE

The Center for Association Leadership

WASHINGTON, DC

The authors have worked diligently to ensure that all information in this book is accurate as of the time of publication and consistent with standards of good practice in the general management community. As research and practice advance, however, standards may change. For this reason it is recommended that readers evaluate the applicability of any recommendations in light of particular situations and changing standards.

ASAE: The Center for Association Leadership
1575 I Street, NW
Washington, DC 20005-1103
Phone: 202-371-0940 (when calling from within the Washington, D.C. metropolitan area)
Phone: 888-950-2723 (when calling from outside the Washington, D.C. metropolitan area)
Fax: 202-220-6439
Email: books@asaecenter.org

ASAE: The Center for Association Leadership connect great ideas to great people to inspire leadership and achievement within the association community.

Keith C. Skillman, CAE, Vice President, Publications, ASAE: The Center for Association Leadership
Baron Williams, CAE, Director, Book Publishing, ASAE: The Center for Association Leadership

A complete catalog of ASAE titles is available online at www.asaecenter.org/bookstore.

Cover design by Beth Lower
Interior design by Cimarron Design, cimarrondesign.com

International Standard Book Number, 10 digit: 0-88034-335-4
International Standard Book Number, 13 digit: 978-0-88034-335-0

Printed in the United States of America.
10   9   8   7   6

Contents

Introduction v

CHAPTER ONE
The Imperative for Change 1

CHAPTER TWO
Overhaul the Governance Model 25

CHAPTER THREE
Overhaul Committees 47

CHAPTER FOUR
Empower the CEO and Enhance Staff 57

CHAPTER FIVE
Rationalize the Member Market 75

CHAPTER SIX
Rationalize Programs, Services, and Activities 95

CHAPTER SEVEN
Bridge the Technology Gap and Build a Framework for the Future 119

CHAPTER EIGHT
Strategies for Success 143

Acknowledgements 153
Suggested Readings 155
Index 157

Introduction

This is a book about change. Radical change.

Whether you are a paid association professional or a volunteer leader, you probably have noticed that today's association model, which was created more than 100 years ago, isn't nearly as effective as it once was. You've likely experienced the challenges firsthand: loss of market share, increased competition for members' time, shrinking revenue sources. And you've seen the irreversible trends that are making the traditional model and accepted practices obsolete: rapid advances in technology, higher member expectations, increased competition, and diverse member markets.

Significant and permanent changes have occurred. Perhaps the biggest are that new competitors now challenge associations and the internet has substantially changed traditional information delivery models. But one thing hasn't changed much: the way associations operate. They govern the same way. They deliver the same services. They communicate the same way. Yet most have experienced tremendous shifts in their markets, their members, and their ability to keep pace in a rapidly changing world.

It's not surprising that despite monumental economic and societal shifts, most associations remain the same. Volunteer leaders dutifully follow in the footsteps of their predecessors. Today's board patterns its functioning on yesterday's board. Today's executive committee continues the processes of yesterday's executive committee. Today's chairman repeats the approach of yesterday's chairman.

Chief staff executives and senior staff have learned their thinking and management styles from their predecessors, their peers, and professional development programs. The archetypal association has been passed down through generations of professional management without much challenge or innovative thinking. And there's a good reason for that: For decades, the traditional association management model worked.

Yet the traditional model for associations doesn't work well in today's environment, and its efficacy will diminish in the future because of rapid changes and the continually shifting landscape. While most associations and professional societies are not in immediate danger, they will struggle if they cling to conventional approaches and structures. They will survive but they won't grow. They will function but without vitality. They will have members but their market share will decrease. They will exist but their influence will decline.

Today's association is in a race for relevance. The track is fast and associations are at risk of falling seriously behind. Worse yet, some are likely to drop out of contention altogether.

So what's an association professional or volunteer leader to do? Soldier on, hoping things will get better? Or challenge the status quo, hoping to keep one's job (if on staff) and one's reputation and position within the organization (if a volunteer leader)?

A changed environment requires an organization to adopt different approaches and methods. When changes in the environment are significant, incremental adjustments are inadequate and radical changes are necessary. Undertaking radical change, by its very nature, must challenge our basic thinking.

This is a book for both professional association managers and the volunteer leaders they work with. It's about fundamental changes in how we operate associations. How we need to lead and manage our organizations. How we should look at our member markets. How we might structure and deliver our programs and services. It's a book about major changes in the way we think about our associations. And it's a book for association leaders—staff and volunteer alike—who want their organizations to thrive, not just survive. It provides a bold, no-nonsense look at the realities of today's marketplace—and what it will take for associations to prosper tomorrow.

Though this book is not grounded in a formal research study, our observations are based on decades of real-world work with associations—from manufacturing to construction, to veterinary medicine and dental, from distribution to agriculture, from auto dealers to healthcare, to banking and electric cooperatives. Our work encompasses a wide variety of challenges, including revamping membership categories, finding funding for innovation, mergers, setting strategic direction, honestly addressing membership declines, and reinventing the culture of an organization. We believe you'll find the narrative both informative and inspiring.

We know that challenging the status quo is one thing. Radically changing it is another. That's why we've not only identified the five radical changes that will energize and reposition your association for better performance, but we've added case studies so that you can learn from what's really working—and what's not. Based on more than 40 years of combined experience working with more than 1,000 associations, we present thought-provoking departures in association governance, management, and strategy. More importantly, we provide a workable guide for how you can implement these changes in your organization—without sacrificing your influence or your sanity.

In addition to providing a look at how actual associations are reinventing themselves to respond to marketplace pressures, this book includes worksheets and questions designed to be used by both seasoned professionals and tomorrow's leaders. These planning tools provide thoughtful and practical approaches to leading your association's revolution, helping you focus not just on the "what," but more importantly, the "why " and "how."

Between the case studies and the worksheets, we believe we've equipped you to begin the race for relevance in your own association. At the minimum, you can use this guide to start a thought-provoking discussion with your leaders. Often, that's where radical change begins—in an informal conversation between staff and or/volunteers. Ideas, once casually batted around, take root and begin to grow. As one conversation leads to another, the merits of change crystallize, paving the way for a new way of doing things.

As consultants, we have a unique vantage point. Each year we talk to scores of staff professionals and interview hundreds of volunteer leaders. We see their frustrations and understand the quandary that confronts them. And we also observe their passionate commitment to making their associations better, stronger, and more relevant to members. It's a spirit we applaud and a force we're committed to encouraging and equipping— one radical change at a time.

Harrison

Mary

CHAPTER ONE

The Imperative for Change

The traditional association operating model—one that's dependent on direction and decision making by volunteers and supported by members—isn't working as well as it once did. Most associations are tradition driven, slow, and risk averse. They are characterized by offerings of a broad range of programs, services, products, and activities. The model is tied to face-to-face interaction through meetings, conferences, conventions, and seminars. And although this is changing, most associations still rely heavily on print for publications, communications, and information delivery.

It used to be that companies automatically joined their trade associations, paid their dues, attended meetings, and volunteered on boards and committees. Professionals naturally joined their professional societies, paid their dues, attended meetings, and volunteered on boards and committees. Life was good. But things have changed.

Now professionals expect value and companies demand return for their investment. Members are extremely busy, constraining their ability to participate and be involved. Competitors offer programs and services once the sole purview of associations. Members have diverse and conflicting interests and a variety of needs and expectations regarding membership—and there's a growing gap in these expectations with each succeeding generation. Technology provides members uncountable alternatives and unlimited, immediate access to products and services now more readily available outside the association environment.

If you scan association publications, you would think all is well. But the fact is many associations are struggling to maintain membership, generate and increase participation, attract volunteers, and compete with alternative service offerings. They are falling behind in the race for relevance.

While most associations and professional societies are not in immediate danger, they will struggle if they cling to conventional approaches and structures. Trade associations will have members, but they will lose market share and influence. Professional societies will have members, but they will lose relevance as their members' average age climbs. If they are not careful, they risk going the way of some community and civic organizations.

It's true the Jaycees still exist. The Shriners are still around. The Rotary is still meeting. The Knights of Columbus, the Kiwanis, and the Lions are all still here. But as Robert Putnam documented in *Bowling Alone,* these community and civic organizations and others like them grew and thrived until the 1960s and 1970s, when they began to experience widespread membership declines. Putnam attributed this collapse to four trends: pressures of time and money, mobility and sprawl, television, and generational differences.

As a result, groups like the Parent-Teacher Association (PTA) lost 500,000 members between 1990 and 1997. The International Lions Club has decreased by roughly 200,000 members from its peak of 570,000 in 1978 (*Houston Chronicle,* Sept. 14, 2009).

Even a race is losing the race! International Soapbox Derby, Inc. (a nonprofit) race attendance has dropped from 50,000 to 15,000 and companies like Levi Straus and Chevrolet have dropped their sponsorships. The *Wall Street Journal* reported that "The Derby's problems have much to do with how the world has changed and how the 75-year-old race hasn't." Square dancing hasn't changed much either, and that's why the United Square Dancers of America dropped from 1 million members in the 1970s to 300,000 today, lamenting that, "Attracting the young isn't easy.... and older dancers complain that young people are too loud and don't respect traditional clothing or music."

The trends affecting today's trade associations and professional societies are similar. As a result, they are in the same race for relevance that many civic and community nonprofits are losing. The associations that will thrive—not just survive—are those that undertake these five radical changes:

- Overhaul the governance model and committee operations;
- Empower the CEO and enhance staff expertise;
- Rigorously define the member market;
- Rationalize programs and services; and
- Build a robust technology framework.

The changes lead to streamlined and nimbler governance; challenged staff who work in true partnership with volunteer leaders; a realistic, well-defined member market that's easier to find and market to; product offerings that are desirable and beneficial for members; and increased financial and human resource capital.

Some associations have attempted the changes above. But often, the attempt is half-hearted. Rather than radical change, the typical association responds through one of the following approaches: The Tinker, The Charade, or The Next Big Thing. None of these approaches is up to the scale of the challenge.

The Tinker. Association executives and volunteer leaders make minor adjustments to their processes or structure. They convert a couple of committees to task forces. They trim a few members from their oversized boards. They make attempts to transition delivery to the internet. They consolidate some meetings and events. They adjust dues and membership categories. But strong traditions and ties to the way it has always been done inhibit making the broader scope of changes that are required.

The Charade. Association staff realizes that conventional practices aren't working, but they don't dare rock the boat. They acquiesce to presidential agendas. They go through the motions with ineffective committees. They enable unqualified volunteer "leaders." They schedule the same meetings. Some acknowledge their plight, and on the side they search for nondues–income opportunities to cover increased operating expenses, knowing that there is little chance of increased membership and dues revenue. Adding to this lack of response are many executives who are approaching retirement with little to gain and much to lose from championing fundamental changes.

The Next Big Thing. There has been a propensity for the association community to latch on to the management innovation du jour. A quick review of association publications and convention speakers confirms this. Perhaps this is at least a tacit acknowledgement that all is not well and that something must be done. Most management fads have at their core some sound, but not necessarily new, practices or approaches. But even if they are applied diligently, their impact is mitigated by being practiced in a fundamentally flawed governance and operating structure.

When addressing the shortcomings of traditional association approaches, consultants and other observers often propose a business model. "Associations should be more businesslike. They should be run like businesses," they say.

Author and consultant Jim Collins disagrees. In a recent monograph on nonprofit management titled, "Good to Great and the Social Sectors," he writes: "We must reject the idea—well-intentioned, but dead wrong—that the primary path to greatness in the social sectors is to become 'more like a business.'"

If the definition of "businesslike" means focusing on producing a profit or driving up the price of the stock, we agree with Collins. But if the definition of "businesslike" means planning strategically, optimizing resources, operating efficiently and consistently, developing and maintaining effective systems, and holding individuals accountable, then it makes sense for organizations to adopt business practices.

It doesn't make any difference if you are a football team, a college or university, a government agency, a corporation, an army, or an association. To perform successfully you must have certain structures and processes. Among other things, all organizations must have priorities and direction. All organizations must align resources with key result areas. All organizations need to hold individuals and departments accountable. All organizations need to optimize resources.

As author and consultant Pamela Wilcox writes in *Exposing the Elephants:*

> The findings of Joseph Galaskiewicz and Wolfgang Bielefeld as they studied a sample of public charities in the Minneapolis–St.Paul area over a 15-year period are illuminating. The results of that study clearly showed that nonprofits that became more businesslike did not suffer as a result and, in fact, experienced significant growth in donations, commercial income, volunteers, and professional staff. The fact that the findings are in a sector where conditions are most resistant to business practices hints at similar and even more favorable findings for the membership sectors. (page 10)

Unlike a business, associations don't have to focus as heavily on the bottom line. Instead, they are challenged with clearly identifying how to help *members* be more successful and determining how to deliver this value in a way that's both convenient and accessible. *More than ever, the way associations become more successful is to help their members do the same.*

The radical changes proposed in this book suggest that associations are no different from any organization in that that they should make the highest and best use of their resources, apply sound management practices that lead to performance, hold individuals and entities accountable, and have clearly defined direction and priorities. They must also discard practices that are no longer effective—usually due to changes in the environment.

Radical change, rather than incremental change, is necessary because the environment has changed considerably and associations have not kept pace. There are six marketplace realities that did not exist 25 years ago that have irreversibly changed the playing field for membership organizations: time, value expectations, market structure, generational differences, competition, and technology. Let's briefly take a look at how each of these issues is affecting association operations and how they have created the race for relevance.

Time

Americans are busier today than ever before. Their days are long. Their calendars are packed. Their schedules are full.

Several trends have converged to create this time-pressed environment. First, it is a documented fact that Americans are working more. *The State of Working America 2008–2009* reports that Americans worked 568 additional hours in 2006 than in 1979—more than workers in most other developed countries. This leads to "work/life conflict" as employees attempt to balance work demands with their desire for leisure and recreational activities as well as time with family and friends. Two-income households are a major contributor to time pressures. According to the U.S. Bureau of Labor Statistics, in 1950 the number of households with two wage earners was under 5 percent; today it is more than 80 percent. In 1960, 28 percent of women with children under the age of 18 in the home worked. By 2009, the number had risen to 71 percent. This results in couples struggling to care for children and attend to household matters once handled by the spouse who worked in the home.

The April 21, 2010, national Funeral Directors Association *Bulletin* reported the results of an association survey in which those who have never served on a committee or board of a national, state, or local funeral service association were asked what keeps them from getting involved. Of those who responded, 41 percent said they "do not have time."

In fact, the CEO of Delta Airlines, who spends 70 hours a week at work, said he would "rather read a book or watch a game" than attend industry social gatherings. He also says he wants to spend time with his wife and children. (*USA Today*, Nov. 22, 2007) Who can blame him?

In addition to the work/life time dilemma, individuals now face the challenge of managing increasingly prevalent technology. What was supposed to make life easier is now a major consumer of time. Work follows individuals home and on vacation. Internet shopping, video games, and other online activities that didn't exist 15 years ago also now devour available time reserves.

This phenomenon's impact is hardly limited to associations. It affects the tourism industry as families take shorter vacations. It challenges the entertainment industry as video games and social networks compete with time to listen to music. It influences compensation in corporate America as more and more employees place a higher value on time than money. It drives the fast food and retail industries because people don't have time to cook meals or shop.

A recent striking example involves Hasbro's board games. Sales of Monopoly were in decline. Hasbro conducted research with their target audience to determine the cause. "We're really, really busy," said a 12-year-old in a Hasbro focus group. To respond to saturated schedules, Hasbro launched new express versions of Monopoly, Scrabble, and Sorry, designed to be played in 20 minutes or less. Express Monopoly has a radical new approach: There's no cash or cards. The properties are listed on 12 dice.

Despite the time crunch, associations continue to operate as if everybody has time on their hands by scheduling regular meetings, expecting major volunteer time commitments, and producing publications or communications that members have time only to skim rather than read in depth. Associations of the future will need to adopt speed dating-like approaches to engagement to stay relevant.

Everybody still has 24 hours each day. That hasn't changed. What has changed is how much Americans are trying to squeeze into those 24 hours. Their "to-do" lists are endless. Their days are long and full. They are leading complex lives, resulting in the necessity of making daily decisions about how they are going to spend their precious time.

While all of this happens around us, associations continue with their time-intensive model. Time to participate on a board or committee. Time to get involved in grassroots political activity. Time to read association newsletters and magazines. Time to attend seminars or conferences. Time to volunteer for a community service program. Time. Time. Time.

These activities assume that average members take the time to inform themselves about the association and its opportunities. The reality is that members are so pressed for time that just getting the attention of a member today is a considerable challenge. Most associations complicate this challenge by trying to communicate too much, resulting in lower, not higher, awareness.

Some association executives lament that members compliment the association on its programs and services and then indicate that they just don't have the time to take advantage of them. These comments often come during exit interviews with members. "Your programs and meetings are great. I just didn't have the time to use them," departing members say.

"I don't have time" is code for "I've got better things to do with my time." Any instance when a member says they "don't have time" is an indictment of the value of the proposed activity or project. People have time for:

- Projects that are meaningful;
- Ideas that help them perform in their work;
- Initiatives that are interesting;
- Causes they care about; and
- Activities that are fun.

Does your association consider the above elements when developing programs or creating volunteer opportunities? If you do, your association will be more successful than those that don't. Consider that trade associations and professional societies have traditionally relied on involved volunteers to populate their boards, committees, and task forces. In some associations (certainly the smaller ones), this volunteer involvement is a key human resource. For years membership organizations have relied on volunteers to keep them abreast of changes in the industry or profession; to develop new programs and activities; and to provide critical horse-power to implement programs. Time pressures have been eroding this resource at the same time that challenges confronting associations have increased. Yet we stick with the old model, hoping that things will get better. They won't.

The Association of Junior Leagues International has come to grips with this trend after a decade when it lost 20 percent of its members. The organization is undertaking a major retooling to stay relevant to the next generation of female volunteers (*Wall Street Journal*, June 18, 2010). "The association of leagues has faced a fiercer competitive landscape for volunteering organizations….and it hasn't adapted to the changing needs of women who are working more and have less time to devote to civic service."

Remember the days when volunteers went through the equivalent of a multiyear career path in the association? They would serve on a committee for a couple of years, chair the committee for a couple of years, serve as a board member for a couple of years, and perhaps even go the officer route for another four to five years. And this could be done first at the state or regional level and then repeated on a national level, resulting in a commitment of 10 years or more.

Now, volunteers are scrutinizing their commitments like never before. They are busy juggling multiple demands. They expect return on their investment of time, and this can be difficult for many organizations to deliver. And more often than not, they have had a volunteer experience that was not productive or efficient and they simply aren't looking for more opportunities to sit through meaningless and unproductive meetings, rubber stamp decisions that have already been made, or spend hours traveling to a meeting that lasts less time than it took to get to.

The time issue is difficult to get a handle on. We can track attendance, open rates on e-newsletters, and volunteer participation levels. But in other areas the time issue is not immediately obvious. It is an invisible but significant force affecting membership organizations. The time famine has reached epidemic proportions and the crunch may well be association enemy number one.

Value Expectations

We observed a subtle change in the 1970s and 1980s: Members started asking what they were getting for their dues.

Increased expectations of associations and professional societies have their roots in consumer behavior. The 1970s and 1980s were decades of significant growth for consumer product and service companies. The buying power and appetite of the 76 million baby boomers created a feeding frenzy. New products and services were introduced at an unprecedented rate. American consumers were presented with an incredible array of choices. In his book *Margin*, Richard Swenson, M.D., notes that in 1978 there were 11,767 items in the average grocery store; today there are more than 24,500 (including more than 186 types of breakfast cereal!). Satellite dishes routinely offer a choice of more than 1,500 movies every month and the number of TV stations available is increasing almost monthly. Cars have more options than ever before. Few needs or wants go unmet. Americans are used to getting what they want when they want it and how they want it.

Such consumer demand has created an environment of significantly increased expectations. As consumers in the 1980s Wendy's commercial asked, "Where's the beef?" association members began asking, "Where's the value?" "Where is the substance?" "Where is the tangible return for the dues check I just wrote?"

Up to this point, membership had been more of an obligation, a duty, something you just did, no questions asked. In the late 1980s Harrison Coerver and Associates asked association members, "Why do you belong to the association?" The answer: "Not really sure. We always did."

For professionals, belonging to their professional society (or more likely, multiple societies) was part of being in the profession. There was, and still is to some degree, an affinity of a CPA to the American Institute of CPAs and a state CPA society; for a physician to belong to the American Medical Association (AMA) and a specialty association, or for engineers, attorneys, scientists, or nurses to be a part of their professional societies. They really didn't think about it much. Belonging to and supporting the professional organization were part of being a professional.

This is no longer the case. In 1965, 75 percent of all physicians belonged to the AMA. Today less than 25 percent do. And worse, those who remain are aging dramatically. What happened? Expectations changed and the AMA didn't pick up on it. Medical specialty groups did get it. (More on this later.)

For companies, belonging to their trade association was part of being in business. Many business owners and CEOs believed it was important to "support the industry." They banded together to work collectively for the "greater good." Though that's still the more important factor, according to ASAE's *The Decision to Join*, "personal benefit" also ranks highly. As things changed, companies grew and management became more sophisticated. Independent, privately held companies gave way to corporations run by professional management. Pressure to perform and attention to expenses brought scrutiny of membership dues. The question became, "What is our ROI for the check we just wrote for trade association dues?" More importantly, the definition of "ROI" changed from one generation to the next and associations are now challenged with recognizing and responding to more varied member needs and wants.

In response to the demand for identifiable ROI, two things happened: Associations added new programs, products, services, and discount plans; and associations began to pursue nondues income. Both may have been flawed approaches for many associations.

Increasing the menu of programs and services was an attempt to increase the value of belonging. The thinking was that the more an association offers with membership, the more value membership has. Wrong. Unused services have no value. Unneeded programs have no value. Uncompetitive products have no value. Association executives took their eyes off the real, though intangible, values and missed the mark. Association consultant Mark Levin asked, "What's all this stuff?" Association executives should have listened to him. More stuff does not necessarily equal more value.

Next, association executives filled seminar rooms for programs about how to generate nondues income. The list of what associations sold to members grew. Boards went along obligingly, since this meant that increasing dues (something strangely abhorrent to boards) would not be necessary. They would have been better off spending their time on creating and communicating the value for the dues dollar and raising dues as necessary instead of offering more "stuff."

Association executives should also have listened to Jim Low, CAE, former president of the American Society of Association Executives, when he challenged the rush to nondues income. He likened this approach to "running around trying to find things to sell members, like operating a convenience store" instead of determining member needs, issues, and problems, and coming up with solutions.

The expansion of services and the increase in nondues offerings had a major negative consequence. It cluttered association communications. The menu of benefits became an unmanageable communications mess. Members now have to hunt through long lists to try to find the value. And most don't even bother to try. Why? Because they're busy!

Bulking up services and increasing nondues offerings was an acknowledgement that associations needed a value proposition that could stand up to increased expectations. They were a response to the need to meet a new market test: return on investment. Unfortunately, instead of increasing the return, many associations just increased the amount of things they offer to members.

It has been at least 20 or 30 years since rising expectations entered the association arena, but some association executives and volunteer leaders are still puzzled. Association articles talk about members expecting value for dues like it is an unreasonable request. Some association executives and volunteer leaders border on indignation at having to justify their dues. Yet the kinder gentler days when members joined because it was the right thing to do are gone and will not return.

Market Structure: Consolidation and Specialization

Trade associations and professional societies serve members who operate in markets. And few, if any, markets have not experienced changes in the way they are composed, structured, and function. In some cases, upheaval in the marketplace is the norm. Yet in the face of fundamental marketplace changes, associations who serve members in these markets continue to offer the same services and function in the same way.

Consolidation is the most common trend in most markets. Either by merger, acquisition, or attrition, a significant percentage of industry revenue is generated by a small percentage of the players. In some cases, a handful of companies represent 50 percent or more of total industry sales.

There is little, if anything, favorable about industry consolidation for a trade association. For starters, it generally results in a smaller member market with fewer potential members. This can at times be offset by new entrants and entrepreneurs who represent new member potential, but the net impact is usually a stagnant universe of potential members as the newcomer growth is offset by consolidation.

Consider the following examples. The top 10 home builders build one out of four homes in the United States today, according to David Crowe, chief economist for the National Association of Home Builders. Just five wholesalers are projected to represent 48.3 percent of total wine and spirits sales in the United States in 2010, according to the April 2010 edition of *Impact* newsletter. According to the Portland Cement Association, three companies control just over 40 percent of all U.S. cement capacity—and they are all foreign-owned. The number of franchised new-car and new-truck dealerships in America has declined from more than 30,000 in the 1970s to fewer than 18,000 today, according to Paul Taylor, chief economist of the National Automobile Dealers Association. We've observed that independent pharmacies have lost major market share to national chain operators and national optometry chains have taken over much of the market once controlled by independent optometrists.

As companies grow to sizes not anticipated years ago, more and more usually fall into the highest dues categories and do not pay dues on revenue above whatever cap currently exists. The trade association is "capped out" of collecting dues from these companies' growth or acquisitions. Stephen Carey, CAE, addressed this challenge in the March 2007 issue of *Associations Now*. He wrote:

> In the last five years, the dues cap issue has been the most disconcerting for trade associations in need of raising dues for large members that have merged or consolidated with one another.... Without a good formula that allows them to capture an equal amount of pre-merge revenue, associations have a most difficult time sustaining or developing capacity for future operations without resorting to significant programs, many of which are off mission and take up staff and volunteer resources.

At the same time, traditional trade association programs and products have little or no value for the larger players. They develop in-house, proprietary training programs with no need for the association's educational seminars. They can negotiate purchasing deals that are equal to or better than association discount programs. They hire their own lobbyists, which can compete with or erode the influence of the association's advocacy efforts. They have the capacity for their own research and development departments and sometimes consider the association's research and development programs competition to their proprietary efforts. In some cases, they develop their own trade shows, which represent direct competition to those of the association. And when they are regional or national in scope, they are less likely to network and exchange experience with competitors than will smaller independents operating in noncompetitive markets.

Consolidation often results in a bimodal distribution of market players, with the very large, national or international companies at one end and the small, independent or niche operators at the other. They have different needs and interests, and this confronts the association with a major dilemma: How do you offer programs or products of value to both? The very services that the smaller company needs are of no interest to the larger company. And the services of interest to the larger company are often too advanced or beyond the scope and finances of the smaller company. How can the association expect the large companies to bear the brunt of the dues when the majority of services are irrelevant to them?

While consolidation has been the biggest challenge for trade associations, the biggest market change for professional societies has been specialization, which is the result of two major factors. First is the growing body of knowledge in all of the professions, and second, the demand in the marketplace for more narrowly focused, specialized services.

Medicine, law, accounting, and all of the other professions are not unchanging. There are new developments, research, approaches, and procedures. It becomes increasingly difficult, if not impossible, to keep abreast of all the developments in the profession's body of knowledge. As a result, professionals focus on specific areas of practice where they can maintain their competency and differentiate themselves in the marketplace. At the same time, consumers, patients, and clients are more knowledgeable and informed about specialized services, thanks to the internet and direct-to-consumer marketing. They know how to seek out and acquire care and services that are focused on their specific needs.

For years, associations and professional societies served members that were more alike than they were different. Now it seems the opposite is the case: Members are more different than they are similar because of the demands of the marketplace.

Consult the directories of professional societies and you will find that the number of specialty and subspecialty organizations has grown steadily in response to this trend as the general professional association has struggled to remain relevant.

Specialists want specialized knowledge. Specialists want to network with other specialists. Specialists want access to suppliers and resources to support their specialized practices. And they will gravitate to the organization or source (nonprofit or for-profit) that best delivers on their need for specific information.

Many associations are like department stores trying to compete with specialty retailers: like Macy's competing with Crate and Barrel for housewares business, with The Limited and Gap for teen apparel, or with Amazon for books. Associations, like department stores, try to be all things to all members rather than focusing on their strengths.

The specialization trend has been unkind to the association incapable of serving an increasingly diverse membership. And the trend continues as specialists are now sub-specializing into narrower and narrower areas of practice. Is it really possible for an association to compete successfully in the general arena when its members are focused more and more narrowly? Instead, perhaps, they would do well to heed the advice of Kenneth Andrews, former editor, *Harvard Business Review*, who wrote, "It is possible, indeed necessary, for an association to develop a *unique* strategy. No matter what the course of the world or the decade, an association is still free, in response to some development or in defiance of others, to devise its own definition of its business and to shape its character as a human organization so that it distinguishes itself, at least in some way, from all its competitors."

Generational Differences

A growing element of membership diversity falls along generational lines because for the first time in history there are five living generations in America. Four of them are working together in the workplace and exist side by side as members and potential volunteers in your association. The five generations are:

- G.I. Generation (born 1901–1926);
- Silents (born 1927–1945);
- Boomers (born 1946–1964);
- Generation X (born 1965–1979); and
- Millennials (born after 1980).

While it's ill-advised to use labeling and stereotypes, it's clear that each generation has its own values when it comes to volunteer service and expectations regarding the return on investment for their dues dollar. They have different ideas about volunteer service, how they prefer to learn, and what types of organizations they choose to be affiliated with.

For example, a 2010 Pew survey found that Millennials are significantly less likely than earlier generations to identify with a religious group, reflecting their waning interest in anything organized. Those in the Silent generation have a traditional work ethic; they live to work. Generation X places personal satisfaction above the commitment to work; they work to live. And while the Silent generation was born to lead and Baby Boomers expect to lead, Generation X overall has less desire to lead. Another key difference is that Generation X is America's least nurtured, least adult-supervised generation, and the Millennials are our most nurtured, most adult-supervised, and most highly scheduled. Because of this, Generation X eschews teamwork and the Millennials value it. Millennials grew up surrounded by technology, so they multitask effortlessly and incessantly— a habit that follows them into meetings as they check their Blackberrys and iPhones even while participating in committee discussions.

These are just a few of the differences. In general, we've seen a trend developing: The traditional association model seems less and less appealing and relevant to each succeeding generation of members. This trend is reinforced when you hear association executives and volunteer leaders lament the decline of younger member engagement and their hopes that the next generation will be more like the generation that placed a higher value on membership and participation.

These perspectives are based on emerging data and over 40 years of association work and observation. In many associations, chapter participation is in decline and there is less interest in participating on committees. Attendance at meetings and conferences is not growing as it once did. With each succeeding generation, there appears to be a growing disconnect with trade associations and professional societies.

Though ASAE research suggests that "the traditional model based on the needs that align with the stages in career development is more useful than generational stereotypes," (*The Decision to Join,* page 4) it seems less important to argue whether the decline in engagement is due to "career stage" or "generational differences." Just ask the membership director of a state dental society about non-join or non-renew rates for younger dentists—or those in the early career stage. Regardless of why it's happening, it's happening.

In ASAE & The Center's research for *The Decision to Join*, a broad sample was asked, "What is your overall attitude toward associations?" Some 43 percent of respondents over the age of 60 gave "very favorable" ratings but only 30 percent of those under 30 years of age gave "very favorable" ratings. The study summarizes:

> The perception of the value of associations increases with age in all but one of the overarching value questions. Asked about the need for associations five years from now, the youngest age group gives an importance rating that surges ahead of all other age groups. This corresponds with other research indicating that this awakening regarding the value of association occurs in the late 20s to early 30s. *The strategic issue for associations is whether they can continue to wait for the surge to take place or, given the proliferation of competing sources of information and networking opportunities, whether they need to improve their benefits in ways that attract the younger much sooner.* (italics ours)

Based on our experience and the opportunity we have to hear the conversations of association leaders during strategic planning sessions, we believe associations need to improve their benefits in ways that attract the younger much sooner. Doesn't this option make more sense than waiting for the surge—mostly because there's no guarantee that the surge will come? We believe that societal changes are enough of a concern that we can't count on history.

The 2006 report "Generations and the Future of Association Participation" by the William E. Smith Institute for Association Research notes, "If there is a meaningful difference between Generation X workers and Baby Boomers, it is not in the propensity to join associations, but rather in their expectations about what membership means and the return it provides."

This research suggests that the generational disconnect can be bridged and declining engagement can be reversed, but only if associations recognize the growing differences in member needs, preferences, and values and do something about it. If they don't, younger people will form their own associations. According to Sarah Sladek, president, Limelight Generations, a Minneapolis-based consulting firm, they already have.

In an April 2008 article in *Association Meetings,* Sladek is quoted, "...the younger generations are forming their own young professional associations out of frustration with the traditional association format. These YPAs, which now number more than 300, are not trade-specific, but instead are organizations where young people of all stripes can get together and share their career development experiences....the growing YPA trend clearly shows that this generation wants to be a part of an association community—although maybe not a traditional association community...."

Since its inception, the Boston YPA has attracted 10,000 members; the Milwaukee version has attained 5,500 members. The Young Nonprofit Professionals Network started in 1997 with one chapter in San Francisco, but it has since added about 20 chapters in the United States. In 2005 a national office opened and a meeting was launched. The organization now has about 10,000 members.

The generational issue is causing a sea change in join rates, volunteer engagement, and the value associations place on programs and services. Vince Sandusky, chief executive officer of the Sheet Metal and Air Conditioning Contractors' National Association (SMACNA), summarizes the situation well: "SMACNA is a strong association, but the next generation of contractors has different definitions of value, different ways of accessing information, different learning processes, and different ways of socializing. SMACNA's traditional structure and processes are not aligned with changing contractor preferences, and the rate of change is accelerating."

Competition

There was a time when associations and professional societies operated with little competition. They had the proverbial sandbox all to themselves. Few association executives would say that this is the case today.

The growth of the number of trade groups and professional organizations has been considerable. The listings of nonprofit and not-for-profit groups in Columbia Books' National Trade and Professional Associations Directory have grown dramatically over the past decade.

The first source of competition has been internal, association versus association. It is curious how most association executives look at this situation. Many are reluctant to refer to these organizations as "competitors." For example, many broad-based associations don't perceive specialty or niche associations as competition and that is a serious mistake. In medicine, for example, physicians are more likely to see value in their area of practice or specialty society than they are the American Medical Association. A manufacturer is likely to see more value in a specialized manufacturing association versus the National Association of Manufacturers. That mindset is understandable. Limited time and limited financial resources result in tougher membership decisions. For many, it makes sense to join the most narrowly focused group.

Associations do compete with one another. They compete for readership of publications and attendance at meetings. They compete for dues and they compete for volunteer participation. Remember, associations serve time-pressed members with high expectations. They are not likely to renew multiple memberships year after year if they aren't getting value. They will narrow their memberships to those with the highest return on investment. And in challenging economic times, the scrutiny of dues expenditures is higher.

Association competition comes from a variety of sources. It generally is not competition from one similar provider. Rather, it is competition from a number of different sources. This makes recognizing and responding to competition difficult for associations.

Competition for readership of association newsletters and magazines is under assault from a seemingly unending and growing source of publications, many of which are now online. Members of associations generally have a backlog of reading stacked on their desks or queued up in their email as they try to keep up.

For-profit trade show companies are another competitive factor. According to Douglas L. Ducate, CEM, CMP, president and CEO of the Center for Exhibition Industry Research (CEIR), in 2009, 23 percent of the 10,000 tradeshows conducted annually in the United States were owned by media companies or entrepreneurs, with the remaining 67 percent owned by associations, as compared to 85 percent owned by associations in 1990.

An indirect competitor for trade show traffic is increasingly the online search. Members can compare products and services from their desks, without out-of-pocket costs of travel and lodging or the impact of absence from the office. CEIR research into the trade show habits of Millenials and Generation X reveals that about two-thirds of those who did not attend all the exhibitions they could have cited convenience and cost as the reason why.

How many providers of continuing education are there for any of the professions? Ask an association executive and he or she will shake his or her head and respond, "There are so many it is almost impossible to count them." On top of this, some providers offer them free as part of their marketing plans. Now that is tough competition!

Associations once were the gatekeepers of industry or professional information. Now independent researchers and in-house studies compete, and often these organizations are more heavily funded, making it difficult for associations to keep up.

In addition, competition for the financial support of suppliers and providers of products and services to members is heating up considerably. These associate or affiliate members are more sophisticated in their marketing efforts and are increasingly looking for integrated marketing packages and reevaluating the return they get on association advertising, sponsorships, and trade show exhibiting. Further, many are investing more heavily in online and mobile media that provide tracking ability not available with more traditional forms of association marketing vehicles. It's no longer "business as usual."

With the growth of internet use, it is likely that new competitors and types of nontraditional competition will grow as it is increasingly easy to enter a market with a website or online deliverable. Brick and mortar buildings are not necessary now that "just-in-time" production and delivery is the name of the game.

Even in the face of the growing and complex nature of competition, most association executives will not have current competitive analyses for their organizations.

Technology

When the internet arrived in the early 1990s, few in the association community realized that the way their organizations would serve their members had changed forever. In the online race, associations were woefully slow out of the starting gate and are laps behind the leaders.

The World Wide Web, as it was known at the time, grew at a rate of 100 percent a year or more during the 1990s, and associations gradually but slowly developed websites and dabbled in electronic communications. If you had a reasonably complete website and offered your newsletter via email by 2000, you were probably ahead of the game as an association.

The inability to capitalize on the internet exposed fundamental organizational flaws. Associations were not organized to respond to this rapidly developing phenomenon. They did not have, or failed to acquire, the necessary expertise to implement technological change. Association staff and volunteer structures were ill equipped to react. But more important, associations lacked the vision and leadership required to allocate the resources and energy needed to exploit the most significant development of the century for their organizations.

Associations paid a steep price for their conservative, tradition-bound natures. Entrepreneurs quickly developed websites, electronic communications, online services, and electronic communities that competed with traditional association offerings. Major communications, information, and technology companies invested billions. And associations stumbled around, developing task forces, distributing RFPs for technological assistance, and trying to figure out how they fit in.

It didn't help that in many cases using the internet meant cannibalizing an existing program or service. An electronic newsletter replaced a printed one. An online educational program competed with a traditional in-person seminar. Associations lacked the will to take risks and often marginalized their efforts by delays in decision making and maintaining traditional delivery methods while slowly introducing online versions of existing information and transactions.

One aspect of association mentality delayed most associations for at least two to three years. If we heard it once, we've heard it a thousand times over the last 15 years: "We can't change the newsletter to online delivery. Some of our members don't have email addresses and some of our members don't even have fax machines yet." The lowest common denominator mentality (a.k.a. "Leave no member behind") crippled associations' attempts to move forward. We would often ask an association board: "Do you have to wait until the last Luddite crawls out of his or her cave and plugs in before we can capitalize on the tool of the century?"

The real cost was the disenfranchisement of progressive members who were adopting technology in their work and life and recognized its value and potential. In their minds, an association that clings to traditional methods is slow, dated, and increasingly irrelevant. "Why aren't they delivering that information via their website?" "Why don't they distribute the newsletter online?" "Why can't I register for the conference electronically?"

In recent years, internet retail sales exploded. Search capabilities mushroomed. Video technology grew rapidly. Wireless technology made access ubiquitous. Thousands of online communities emerged. But in associations, attention and effort lagged. Association websites had marginal utility and many were static. Systems were not integrated. Online initiatives were underfunded. Technology plans were lacking. Innovation was absent. Few if any associations asked, "What can we do that was impossible before the internet arrived to deliver value to members?"

Associations thought they were getting caught up until Web 2.0 arrived in 2005. This one example demonstrates the cost of years of inadequate internet strategy and execution by associations: the social network. We will look back at the mid-2000s as the beginning of the end for associations as the hub of professional or business networking. In the last three years, the likes of MySpace, Facebook, and LinkedIn have captured the online networking space at the expense of association networking, and it is unlikely that associations will recapture this position, since the online environment changes so rapidly. As of this writing, 96 percent of Millennials have joined a social network. Facebook added more than 200 million users in less than one year. One in six higher education students are enrolled in online curriculum. With numbers this staggering, associations are foolish not to invest in the technology necessary to help them connect with both members and potential members. Yet many have a major job of catch up. For some it is a gap that needs immediate attention.

Summary

So what are association executives or volunteer leaders to do, given the fundamental changes that confront them in the areas of time, value, market structure, generational differences, competition, and technology? Make the five radical changes to the traditional model of association structure and processes outlined in this book and you'll be equipped to address all six challenges.

It is critically important that the proposed radical changes for associations be undertaken in sequence. They have been presented in the order that they should be pursued, beginning with addressing governance. While the changes required in association governance are the most difficult, it is essential that they be achieved first. If not, there will be little, if any, chance of making meaningful progress on the other changes.

The suggested governance changes anticipate the remaining four recommended changes that are outlined herein. Knowing the radical changes ahead in thinking about member market/programs and services and technology will provide important insights into the competencies that will be required to govern the organization, particularly in the initial years of transition.

After governance, precisely defining the association's optimum member market is a prerequisite for rationalizing and aligning programs, services, products, and activities. You cannot make these decisions until you know the member that the association will be serving. Once you more fully understand your members, it's easier to determine how to bridge the gap in leveraging technology in order to effectively offer relevant programs, services, and products. We do not advocate adopting technology for technology's sake, but we do know technology decisions are vastly improved when you know what fits the programs and services you will be delivering.

The sequence of change is of major importance in a successful transformation. First, we start with the right governance. Next, decisions regarding the member market that will lead to the right program and product mix. And finally, determination of the best technologies to deliver the elements of the benefit package. These are radical changes but they can be accomplished one step at a time. Read on to find out how.

Overhaul the Governance Model

The changes required in association governance are the most important and most difficult. They must be achieved first. If not, there will be little, if any, chance of making meaningful progress on the other changes.

The governance traditions, structure, and processes in most associations can be the biggest impediment to effecting change. But once the association has a capable leadership team in place, constructive change can come quickly.

Believe it or not, an association can be effectively governed by a board of five, not including the CEO. Yes, five.

Most association boards do not effectively govern or lead their organizations. They waste time. They underutilize the talent and abilities of their directors. They are reactive. And in the biggest indictment of the association profession, they continue to micromanage staff. How can the profession defend decade after decade of micromanaging boards with little or no improvement?

Instead of boards being an asset, they are a liability. Millions of hours of association staff time each year are squandered on unproductive board activities. The cost of the care and feeding of board members is immense. Call an association office the week before its upcoming board meeting. In a small association, the entire staff is focused on preparations for the meeting.

In a large association, most of the senior management is consumed. With four meetings a year, the average association allocates a month a year to board meeting preparation alone! And this doesn't count the two or three days of follow-up activity and recuperation after the meeting.

If your association could concentrate its entire staff or senior management team on one thing for a solid month, what could it accomplish? Probably something significant. And that is the cost of managing a large board.

Preparing for board meetings is only a small percentage of the staff time, energy, and effort required to support board members throughout the year. And the larger the board, the more resources required. Other management tasks range from handling requests for information to pleas for better hotel rooms at the convention or seats at the awards dinner.

The problem with most boards is simple: They are too large and they are not composed for performance. Large boards are not effective. They are cumbersome. They are slow. They are full of political entanglements. They are difficult to manage. And they generally continue to get larger.

The more we analyze board functioning, the more convinced we are that large boards are a very real problem. They don't govern. They don't lead. They are an encumbrance and costly. They don't add value. Instead of contributing to the organization, they are a costly drain on the association's valuable staff and resources.

But the biggest consequence of a large board is disengagement. The larger a board gets, the less engaged the individual director tends to be. Psychologists call this "social loafing"—when individuals fail to take personal responsibility for the group's actions and instead rely on others to take the lead.

When the board is small, directors know that their presence and attention are important. When the board gets to be 20 or 30 members, missing a meeting or being absent from a conference call won't be as noticeable. At 40, you need microphones at the meetings so that directors can hear each other. And we have observed that at 50 members, some members begin to read *USA Today*, text, or read emails at the board meetings.

There is a phenomenon regarding board size that we have observed: As board size increases, a dynamic places authority and control into a smaller group. As board size grows beyond the mid-teens, the executive committee comes into play. This happens in one of two ways. In the first, the officers of the association become frustrated with the unproductive and futile dysfunction of the larger board and assume authority for decision making. As a smaller and more effective group, they deal with the issues and make a recommendation for board action (also known as rubber stamping). In the other scenario, the large board becomes frustrated with their unproductive and futile dysfunction and delegates the decision making to the officers. "We are tired of fooling with this. You sort this out and come back to us with a recommendation."

This separation of power produces an unproductive tension between executive committees and boards that results in more unproductive board and staff time trying to resolve the ensuing conflicts. Boards complain that the executive committee is usurping their responsibilities. Executive committees complain that their boards are indecisive, reactionary, and in the way of progress. Emails fly. Complaints are lodged. Staff intervenes. Consultants are retained. Hours of debate and wasted time—all because of a large board.

But the point is this: There is an organizational dynamic at work that will, over time, place authority and control into a smaller group. Years ago we came across the epitome of a governance structure that vividly demonstrates the dynamic of moving to a small, workable group to govern. A national organization's board continued to get larger. As it grew to over 20 members, the executive committee was formed. Then as the board grew to over 50, the executive committee increased to over 20. As the larger executive committee got bogged down, a management committee of six was formed that could effectively deal with decision making. The board continued to grow, the executive committee continued to grow, and now the management committee increased to 20. As the management committee got bogged down with its size, an operating committee of six was formed. Group dynamics drove the changes that repeatedly resulted in the appointment of a smaller, more effective group.

The lesson should not go unnoticed: Large boards are not effective. In reality, almost all associations and professional societies are actually governed by the officers or an executive committee of about five individuals.

Sources of Large Boards

Large boards come from various sources or rationales, none of which result in effective governance or leadership.

Many boards are composed of representatives elected or selected from geographic regions. The rationale is that members, for example, in the Southeast have different needs and interests than those in the Midwest and these needs and interests require representation on the board. If challenged, most would be hard-pressed to articulate what those differences are. In this scenario, geography matters, more than board leadership, competence, or ability.

The consequences of this approach to board composition are considerable. First, board members take a parochial view to issues. "In my part of the state (country or region) we see it this way." Elected or appointed directors feel compelled to focus on the perceived differences from their locale when they should be governing in the best interests of all members.

The other downside of geographic composition is the impact on the quality of directors. Let's say the board must have a representative from Missouri. We have come across scores of situations where there is only one member from Missouri interested in serving on the board, so that person serves on the board, term after term, regardless of leadership ability or competence. At the same time, several well-qualified members from Florida may be interested in serving and can't. Because the group already has a director from Florida, they are now saddled with that incompetent director from Missouri who likes to travel to board meetings and network with cronies.

A subset of this approach is where all state, regional, or local chapter presidents have a seat on a national board. As the chapter network grows, so does the board. And now you have directors that (a) serve only one term and (b) are doing double duty as a national director and chapter president. (This is like being a mayor or governor at the same time you are serving as a U.S. Senator!) How effective can an individual be in both roles simultaneously?

Many large boards are composed with representation allocated to special interests or constituencies. The rationale here is that these interests and constituencies can be served only by having one of their own on the board. Special interests are what matters, not leadership, competence, or ability.

The consequences of this approach to board composition are also considerable. First, these directors feel a burning compulsion to articulate their differences from all other interests and constituencies. They often become single-issue oriented and rarely participate in discussions that are not relevant to their constituencies. It can become almost comical: The only time they speak at board meetings is in relation to their special interest, regardless of the topic at hand.

Secondly, the concept of specialty representation inevitably leads to a larger and larger board. If special interest A gets a seat on the board, then why not special interest B? And now what about special interests C, D, E, F, and G? Believe it or not, in one large professional society, the only member not represented on the board was the average, typical professional! All the board seats were allocated to special interest constituencies.

Finally, the assumption that a representative of a special interest can articulate and convey what the constituency needs can be flawed. Case in point: A construction association was struggling with how to reach the next generation of contractors. It happens that they have a seat on the board for the president of the young contractors' council. During the board discussions, they logically turned to him and asked, "What can we do that will attract young professionals to the association?" He shook his head and said, "I just don't know." So much for special interest representation. There are more effective ways, including surveys and focus groups, to determine the needs of different constituencies or segments in your membership.

The "good old boy" system also contributes to large boards. Long-standing directors serve term after term. Term limits don't exist, aren't enforced, or are ignored. The board gets larger as directors hang on to their seats. It becomes apparent that the board could use some "new blood," but no one wants to go off the board to make room for the next generation of leadership. So, director positions are added and the board gets larger.

The process for identifying new directors usually goes something like this: "Does anybody on the board know someone who would make a good director?" Or, "Who do you know that would be interested in being on the board?" This, of course, assumes that current directors know what "makes a good director." It is board composition by who you know rather than what potential board members know and bring to the table.

Another question asked often by nominating committees is, "Whose turn is it?" In this case, being a director is a function of how much time an individual has been willing to commit to serving on committees or volunteering for projects or simply hanging around at meetings. In today's time-pressed environment, one should be suspicious of people who have this kind of time available. Isn't their presence at their own company, firm, or practice important? If not, why not? In this case, when ability isn't considered, the nominating committee might as well ask, "Who's alive and kicking?" or "Who can we get to say yes?" The resulting quality of volunteers may be the same in either case.

Still another practice in some trade associations that leads to a large board is providing a seat on the board for every member company. Trade association memberships can be relatively small, particularly in an era of continuing consolidation. So with 30 or 40 companies as members, why not give each company a director so that everybody has a voice?

The last contributor to larger boards is the provision that all past presidents or chairmen continue to serve on the board. Each year the board increases by one. And over time, this ensures that the board ages and an increasing percentage of directors retire, leaving the association's governance in the hands of individuals no longer active in the industry or profession that they are charged to govern.

In regard to boards elected by the members-at-large, one need only to look at the percentage of members who voted. And that doesn't address the fact that those who do rarely know the qualifications of the candidates they vote for.

Boards are larger than they need to be for many reasons. But large boards have a lot in common: They don't govern well; they don't optimize the potential of the individual directors; and the time required to support them has a high opportunity cost. Why do we tolerate this inefficiency?

Why Do Individuals Want to Be on Boards?

Before we move to the radical board change required, let's touch on a rarely discussed factor in board performance: the motivation to be a director. Why do people want to be appointed or elected to boards? According to ASAE's *The Decision to Volunteer,* individuals volunteer for a variety of reasons, including helping others, creating a better society, civic duty, a desire to make a difference, to learn new skills, and a need for affiliation, among other reasons. We believe these can be summarized in three categories:

Altruism. The motivator here is an unselfish desire to serve and advance the best interests of the industry or profession. This often occurs when successful business people want to "give something back" to the industry or profession from which they have benefited.

Self-interest. The motivator here is personal gain or an advantage for the company, practice, or firm that the director represents. The benefits can include enhanced market visibility and credibility, high-level business contacts, professional referrals, and networking as well as access to valuable market or professional information.

Ego. The motivator here is self-importance or self-esteem, having something that looks good on the résumé.

We are convinced that each individual is motivated by all three factors, but the degree that each plays a part in the motivation is different and subject to change over time.

At the beginning of a meeting of a professional society, each new director was asked to give the rest of the board a self-introduction and to explain what had motivated them to pursue a seat on the board. One new director said, "I will be very straightforward with you. One reason I agreed to serve is because it will be good for my practice. I will make contacts. My credibility is enhanced. It will be a positive item on my résumé. Secondly, I owe this association for the support and assistance it gave me when I started my practice over 20 years ago. And I believe it is a good organization that adds value and I think I can play a small part in improving its performance or strengthening its ability to add value. Finally, part of it is pure ego. You asked me to be on the board, and that acceptance means something to me personally."

How many directors would score the highest on the altruism scale? There are many whose self-interest and ego account for 95 percent of their motivation. We all have egos and self-interest, but the higher the impact of altruism is, the better the director. Yet most selection processes don't even bother to ask potential directors why they want to serve.

The Small, Competency-Based Board

The first and most important of the five radical changes is to overhaul the size and composition of the board of directors. All other changes are substantially dependent upon this first move. If this idea seems ludicrous or impossible, please don't stop reading. The remaining changes have plenty of merit of their own. Plus, as you work through the book, you'll begin to see how relevant associations create a culture where change is possible—first by questioning, then by reviewing related data, debating the value of change, and using a matrix system that we outline in later chapters. It's entirely possible that a discussion held now won't bear fruit for years. Even if your organization doesn't end up making the radical changes outlined in this text, you'll benefit from having discussed the possibility and introducing a new way of thinking for your current and future leaders.

As noted, when boards get large, pressure builds to get decision making into fewer hands. As Richard Pozen wrote in an op-ed piece in the *Wall Street Journal* (Dec. 21, 2010), "Psychologists such as Harvard's Richard Hackman suggest that groups of six or seven are the most effective at decision making. Groups of this size are small enough for all members to take personal responsibility for the group's actions. They also can take decisive action more quickly than a large board." Our five-member board, plus the executive director, meets this suggested size of six.

Boards naturally gravitate to a smaller, workable group like an executive committee. As this tends to be the case in almost all boards we have encountered, why do associations need the baggage of the rest of the board? They do not add any value, and in fact, they add cost. In reality, almost all associations are already operating with a five-member board.

The board we recommend is based on competency, not geography, special interests, or who you know. Most associations select their board members with the flawed assumption that anybody can govern.

Governing, however, is difficult. To succeed, you need a good under-standing of what competencies are needed on the board. In the competency arena, a potential director has to pass the leadership and governance test. Here are questions to move thinking from "Whose turn is it?" to "Who demonstrates the most promising leadership?"

- Do candidates have basic leadership skills? (Not an ability to manage, but to lead.)
- Do they have at least a three-to-five-year horizon in their thinking?
- Can they guide the association into the future?
- Can they effectively direct the association's resources to achieve its goals and objectives?
- Do they have the ability to inspire and empower others?
- Can they build teamwork among peers with different needs and interests?
- Can they demonstrate their leadership abilities, not just articulate them?
- What have they done to show that they can move people and an orga-nization in the right direction?
- What examples can they give where they have been able to cultivate productive teamwork?
- In what instances have they skillfully and creatively directed resources to accomplish objectives?

The director identification and screening process must be a disciplined approach that ensures that candidates have proven leadership ability, not just agreeable personalities, or charisma, or the ability to say the correct things.

The second test is the governance test. Governing is challenging and a candidate should have a track record of performing in a governance capacity. The following questions help determine skill in governing:

- Do the candidates know what it means to govern?
- Do they understand the duties and functions of a board and the role of a director?
- Do they know the duties of care, loyalty, and obedience?
- Do they know that governing is much more difficult than managing?

- Can they demonstrate how they have governed appropriately and effectively in the past?
- Can they give examples of how they have exercised their duties of care, loyalty, and obedience?
- Can they give instances where they have been able to elevate their peers from micromanaging to governance?
- What have they done to show that they can make judgments in the interests of the entire membership and deal with conflicting interests?

The process of selecting the five directors should be critical and is guided by an understanding of what competencies will be needed to govern the association and direct it effectively into the future.

The first step is to analyze the major challenges and opportunities for the association in the next five to 10 years. What high-impact trends or developments will affect the membership, the members' market, or the association's environment? This analysis should be conducted with great care. Existing research and studies should be referenced. Recognized experts or specialists should be consulted. Member or leadership surveys should be considered.

Once the challenges and opportunities have been accurately identified, it's easier to determine what competencies will be needed on the board, not in terms of technical skills but in high-level knowledge and understanding.

For example, if the association's leadership and staff see technology emerging as an increasingly important delivery mechanism for services, information, networking, and education, who in the membership can bring a level of knowledge and understanding of its potential and how it might be exploited? Not a techie or "propeller-head" but someone who is aware of general technological trends and applications and how the association might adopt or capitalize on them. For example, the Oklahoma Dental Association took advantage of the fact that one of its board members is highly advanced in the use of technology—so much so that he lectures on the topic. When it was time to construct a new building several years ago, the association used the member's knowledge to build a facility that includes videoconferencing, the ability to receive satellite signals, and internet access throughout the building, none of which was standard at the time. The high-tech office allows the association to more fully address member needs, effectively handle general operations, and provide in-person and distance learning as well as enabling council and committee members to participate in meetings without always having to be physically present.

If an association sees increased inter-organizational collaboration, joint ventures, or possible mergers in its future, who has relationships that might be leveraged or contacts that would be helpful? Who has the organizational political savvy that would be an asset in representing us in joint venture discussions?

If the organization's financial situation will be complex, who brings a good understanding of financial matters? This is one area of knowledge that executive committees generally recognize. There are many instances of one individual's continuing for several years in the treasurer position because that person possesses an understanding of the numbers and can guide the rest of the leadership in making financial decisions. A critical contribution this person can make is a good understanding of how the association's resources are allocated and how they might be reallocated to improve performance in key result areas.

If programs and services are dated, you may need someone who understands the challenges of developing marketable products in a competitive environment, someone who has experience in developing a concept into a revenue-generating product, someone who has an understanding of how to abandon obsolete activities and reallocate resources to new, emerging services.

One position that deserves consideration is the visionary, an individual who has a good grip on the trends and developments that are taking place in the industry or profession and has a sense of where it is going, someone who has taken an extraordinary interest in the industry or profession and has made a hobby of studying and analyzing it at a high level. Not only can visionaries see the future, they are often able to help others do the same. And, perhaps ever more valuably, they can help generate excitement about future possibilities.

Let's assume that your association has conducted its analysis on the high-impact areas and has come to the conclusions outlined in the above paragraphs. You are now prepared to initiate your search for five directors: one with an understanding of technology, another with relationships and political savvy, one who is financially competent, another with product development knowledge, and finally, a visionary.

A final thought on the competency-based director selection process: We don't believe all board members have to be association members. An association may not have a member with the necessary leadership, governance experience, or competency. Instead of leaving the position open or filling it with someone unqualified, the association should look outside its membership for the right individual. While not common, there are instances where associations have successfully recruited outside directors with a relationship with the industry or profession. According to Gary Bolinger, CAE, president of the Indiana CPA Society:

> We have had outside directors since 1999. We actually have two in order to provide some continuity for that role of "public member." We created these public member positions on our board to enhance diversity of thought, to bring us an outside perspective. All too often, association boards, no matter how "diverse" they are, are all rooted in the same industry or profession. The outside view that our public members bring can be very valuable in causing the board to look at an issue or opportunity from a different perspective.
>
> Over the years, our public member has been attorney, a banker, the CEO of a "think tank," a former state legislator, the senior vice president of a nonprofit and most recently, a consultant in marketing and sales for professional service firms. Our public members have made significant contributions over the past 10 years. Each person has brought a unique and very valuable perspective to the table.
>
> I am often asked, "But why do they serve?" Well, it isn't the money. While we do compensate them modestly—$500 per meeting—these public members of our board have told me they gain value. They learn about organizational processes and governance; they make new contacts and expand their networks; they get a different perspective; and they feel like it is one more way to "make a contribution." They serve for a variety of reasons. And it is interesting to note that we have never been declined by a prospective outside director. So they must perceive value and an opportunity to contribute. I just wish we had made the decision earlier to add public members to our board.

Compare a competency-based team with a geographically-based board, a special interest-based board, a "good old boy" board, or a "Whose turn is it?" board. There's a vast difference. As an association chief staff officer, which would you rather have? As a volunteer leader, which board would you prefer to serve on?

One caution: Don't confuse board competencies with staff competencies. In small, heavily volunteer-oriented associations, you may need some hands-on input from directors in their area of knowledge. But in associations with reasonably sized staffs, you don't want to replicate competencies on the board with those that exist on staff. They should complement each other, not duplicate or compete with each other. In general, directors' knowledge or understanding in their area should be at a high, conceptual level—not a tactical or implementation level. They should be focused on the potential or possibilities in their areas, not implementation.

An additional caution: Safeguards must be in place to ensure that a competency-based director doesn't participate like a special interest director. They must understand that as a member of the leadership and governing team that their input and participation on all association matters is critically important. A small board doesn't have anyone to blame for missed opportunities, failed initiatives, or glaring mistakes. All five directors must be fully on board and fully engaged.

The selection process has to be rigorous. It has to be disciplined. It has to be taken seriously. It can't be impulsive, rushed, or conducted cavalierly.

An outside professional should be retained to organize and guide the identification and vetting process. While we're not aware of this practice in the association arena, search professionals are commonly used to identify and screen corporate directors.

Many associations would not think twice about hiring a search consultant to provide professional assistance in identifying and selecting a new CEO for the association. The expense of doing so is more than offset by reducing the risk of making a costly hiring mistake. Why do we not think of directors the same way? What is the cost of appointing an ineffective director to the board, particularly if you have adopted a five-member board? Why will we invest a considerable amount in the search for our chief staff executive while simply asking "Who do you know?" or "Whose turn is it?" when it comes to selecting a director with leadership and governing responsibilities?

If an association can afford thousands of dollars for board-related travel, meals, and meeting expenses, it can afford professional search assistance for director selection. As a matter of fact, if an association has a large board and downsizes to five competency-based directors, it could redirect the costs associated with the large board and use those resources to fund the search consultation services for directors. In our opinion, it would be money better spent.

Radical Changes for Boards

Board downsizings are not uncommon. However, most downsizings stop short. The size of the board will be reduced from 36 to 16 members, as was the case with the American Society of Association Executives in 2007. The National Rural Health Association reduced the size of its board from 40 to 15 in the 1990s. The National Congress of Parents and Teachers reduced the size of its board from 87 members to 28. All are significant accomplishments. But most downsizings don't go far enough.

If you are going to go through the considerable time and effort, politics, and taking on years of tradition, you might as well go for a down-sizing that will make a major difference. Once you have the conceptual agreement, why stop at 18 or 16 members? You might as well go all the way to our recommended board size of five.

Downsizing a board is one of the most significant governance challenges, right up there with eliminating micromanagement. While a daunting undertaking, it can be accomplished. The following nine tips are critical to getting the job done.

1. Do not underestimate how difficult this will be. It is going to take years to accomplish. You need a plan that will pace and sustain the effort. You need to be prepared to accept setbacks. You need to know when to lay low with the effort, and you need to know when to accelerate your implementation. As you will see with the following steps, years may be required, but the results will be worth it.

2. Know that, few, if any, directors want to lose their seats on the board. The first step is to eliminate the first line of resistance by making it clear that everybody on the board will serve out their terms. No one currently on the board will be asked to depart prematurely. Nobody will have to give up a seat. Terms will run their course, but as each term comes to an end, the vacant seat will not be filled. Board members are more likely to surrender someone else's future seat on the board than to give up their own.

3. It's important to build your case carefully and don't be shy about the first draft. Make it brutally honest and apolitical. Your case for change should address the following areas:

- Instances where your large board has missed an opportunity or bungled a situation.

- Demonstration of how a small, competency-based board could have better capitalized on opportunities or more effectively addressed situations. For example, let's say your board took more than a year to approve a new revenue-generating program or service. What was the cost of a lost year of revenue? What competitors entered the market while your board deliberated and postponed?

- Graphic depiction of how your large board consumes valuable staff time. Back this up with examples and estimates of the hours of staff time consumed and opportunity cost resulting from the care and feeding of directors versus adding value to membership.

- Proposal about how the resources now spent on board support could be reallocated to important and productive efforts and what the potential impact would be.

- A summary of where directors have not performed: missed meetings, conference calls, and committee assignments; poor or no follow up to assigned projects; and failure to prepare or participate.

- Demonstration of instances where your board, in spite of its large size, has lacked skills, knowledge, or competencies that the association needed for guidance or direction on key issues.

4. Draft your plan. Develop a step-by-step strategy with timelines. Remember, it will require all directors serving out their terms. It will probably require at least two phases, but lay out your approach.

5. Take your case and plan to a current or incoming chief elected officer who has experienced the flaws of the current system. This person will be someone who is an insightful leader, understands the association's politics but is not immersed in them, and is respected by the rest of the leadership. Pick this individual carefully. If you can't make this first sell, your prospects for success are at best significantly diminished and, at worst, potentially doomed.

6. If your first champion agrees with your assessment and plan, then you can expand to a small core of additional leaders. They may be officers or board members, a past president, or a major player in the industry or profession. You will probably need a mix of those currently serving and others not on the board. But they must be knowledgeable about the association, committed to its purpose and its future, and respected by their peers.

With this core group you can take your unvarnished case and redraft it into a politically correct plan to restructure the association's governance.

7. Identify the individuals who will stand in the way. Use your core group to help you identify who opponents might be. Make a list. Rank them in terms of their ability to mount resistance to the change. Know who will just get in the way and who has the potential to completely sabotage the process. Analyze their motives. Why would they be opposed? How will they attack the proposed redesign? How can you respond to their pushback? How can they be neutralized or their opposition weakened? You may get a surprise or two, but you and your core leader leadership team should be able to identify almost all the opposition.

8. Understand concerns and be prepared to respond. There will be concerns and pushback. Some will be based on "how we've always done it" or simple aversion to change. Others will be based on politics or self-interest. But there will be legitimate questions, and you should be prepared with solid answers. Here are five good questions that are likely to be asked and our thoughts about how to respond:

- **How would you reconcile the membership's "ownership" of the association with the radical change to a five-member board?**
  We believe that the five-member, competency-based board will

significantly strengthen the association and the value of membership, and that members would rather "own" a strong association with high value than a weak one with marginal value. In addition, there is an assumption that a member's "ownership" is somehow a function of how many individuals there are on the board. Let's be honest. Ask a member-at-large how many members there are on the association's board. Ask that member to name more than one current director. At best, they will guess at both questions. We believe "ownership" is more a function of relevance than how many are on the board.

- **What about diversity? Won't a five-member board limit diversity of perspectives and opinions?**

  While it will take some hard work, a five-member board and diversity are not mutually exclusive. A five-member board could conceivably cover the competencies the association needs for optimal governance and still address diversity, for example, in the areas of gender, ethnicity, youth, size, and geography. The more important issue is keeping the board attuned to the diversity of needs, interests, and circumstances among members. This requires systematic research, outreach, and dialogue—things that are not exclusive to large boards. A larger board is not necessarily representative of the needs and opinions of members-at-large. Often, the more involved the volunteer, the more out of touch that member is with the rank and file.

- **What about the loss of professional fulfillment and networking that board members value?**

  The role of the board is to govern the association, to guide its efforts and activities in the best interest of the members. The valuable, high-level networking that board members enjoy is a byproduct of their governing role as is the forum to debate industry or professional issues. Unfortunately, some directors place more priority on the byproducts of networking and debate versus their core governing responsibilities. Governing is a difficult and challenging but vital function for associations, more so today and in the future than in the past. Networking and dialogue is relatively easy and there are multiple options to provide it to leaders in the profession or industry. For example, an industry or profession "summit" might replace the networking and high-level discussions previously enjoyed by the larger board.

- **Won't it be easier for one of five directors to advance a special agenda?**
  Not if the rigorous selection process we propose is followed. And if a special-interest or self-interested director slips through the cracks in the system, we believe a smaller, stronger board is more likely to confront this individual than a large board because it's less uncomfortable to do so in a smaller group. Consequently, we would argue that a larger board is much more vulnerable to political maneuvering than a small one.

- **We already have more members willing to serve than volunteer opportunities in the current structure. Now that imbalance will be exacerbated. How do we deal with this?**
  Interest in governing and ability to govern are two different things. And our earlier analysis shows there are multiple motivations to serve on boards. But if you assume that your volunteer "bench" is deep with talent, think of how strong your committee and task forces will be. Think of how your grassroots advocacy efforts, your fundraising campaigns, your community outreach, or social responsibility initiatives will be. And if the volunteer pool is not attracted to these opportunities, one must ask why their sole interest is being on the board.

9. Picture the promise. People will give something up for a gain or benefit elsewhere. "If we give up our traditional board structure, what do we get in return?" Identify a short list of initiatives with high impact and commit to achieving them in a very short time given the change to the five-member, competency-based board.

Though working toward radical change isn't without pitfalls, streamlining governance at both the board and committee levels enables the other necessary changes we outline later. We'll address committee changes in the next chapter.

Radical Change: Moving to a Five-Member Board

ASSOCIATION: New Jersey Veterinary Medical Association (NJVMA)

BUDGET: $450,000

NUMBER OF STAFF MEMBERS: Managed by Professional Management Associates (an association management company)

NUMBER OF MEMBERS: 1,000

CASE STUDY:

The New Jersey Veterinary Medical Association (NJVMA) has done what few before it have: moved from geographically-based board representation to competency-based *and* decreased the size of its board to five members. Both changes are the result of a close look at the reality of association management and governance today: Volunteers are pressed for time and associations are more complex than ever. Many are moving from operations-focus to setting strategic direction and evaluating overall performance, mirroring for-profit boards more than a traditional association board. Rick Alampi, NJVMA executive director, doesn't mind. In fact, he says, "If you're not changing the governance and structure of your association, you're going to run the risk of becoming irrelevant."

Alampi serves as the executive director of six associations, including NJVMA. None are still represented geographically or by special interests. All have recognized the value of finding the best and brightest leaders, rather than those who happen to live in a certain region or represent a special interest. He says, "I simply tell the volunteers I work with, 'If you picked a baseball team by zip code, you may end up with nine catchers.' They get that. And I follow up by saying, 'If we've got three superstars that live in the same town, why wouldn't we want the three superstars?'" Now, instead of recruiting volunteers based on special interest or location, leaders are recruited based on a list of core competencies compiled by the association. These include vision, resilience, flexibility, open-mindedness, passion, and commitment to both the profession and the association.

The change to a competency-based board took 18 months and was underway when the reduction in board size was initiated, also the result of a hard look at reality. The truth for NJVMA is that three or four people drove board meetings—and many of the others on the board were unprepared. "You've seen it," says Alampi. "We'd create these board books and we'd send them out three weeks ahead of time, and they didn't even put on the sham of pretending. They'd actually be opening the envelopes at the board meeting. When I pointed this out to the board, they acknowledged that they don't have time and that often, they don't understand the issues."

Though the change to a smaller board meant displaced volunteers, some moved to the association's foundation board while others are now involved with a regional veterinary conference. Others were happy to simply end their service to the association.

The NJVMA board is now elected by the membership as a whole from a slate of at-large candidates. The five-member group elects its own president and treasurer and meets four times a year. Meetings last less than two hours.

Alampi admits that the move isn't for every association. Some of the groups he manages are too social for the change. "That's a big obstacle when I talk to other execs about this," says Alampi. "Their boards are very social and they wouldn't want to give up their friendships and everything else that they have. But they're approaching it not on the basis of what's good for the association, but what's good for them."

Alampi acknowledges that there's a high level of trust between him and the NJVMA board, which made it easier to steer the group through the change, since consensus is key to navigating the white waters of change. Alampi advises association executives proposing change to, "Get some of your trusted volunteer leaders together...have dinner, and just talk to them about it. And you'll get a feel for it. And if, after talking to three or four of them, it's all negative, then just give it up. If they think it's intriguing, at that point take it to the next level. Bring in more leaders."

Smart executives know that the more support you have the easier change becomes—whether you're changing board composition or rethinking your member market. It's a theme you'll see repeated in the case studies throughout this book and one worth paying attention to in your own organization as you measure your association's readiness for change—radical or otherwise.

Chapter Two, Case Study 2

Radical Change: Moving to a Competency-Based Board

ASSOCIATION: American Animal Hospital Association (AAHA)

BUDGET: $11 million

NUMBER OF STAFF MEMBERS: 70–75

NUMBER OF MEMBERS: 40,000

CASE STUDY:

In addition to its board, the American Animal Hospital Association previously had regional team members designated to help with grassroots activities for the association. That's how it was supposed to work, anyway, though it rarely did. John Albers, former executive director, recalls, "This component of our governance structure was costing us a lot of money and not delivering much in the way of results." Further complicating the problem was that these regional teams produced future board members for the association, whether the individuals had been effective or not. "Our board was one that was based more on seniority and 'whose turn is it?' than competency."

When a task force charged with looking at the association's governance recommended moving to a competency-based board, it addressed other changes as well, including eliminating the regional teams, shrinking the number of committees, and reducing the length of board terms from three years to two. The result? Cost savings to the association because the biannual meetings of the regional teams were eliminated and a much more effective and strategic board, according to Albers.

The association now has a Leadership Identification Committee (LIC) assigned to identify, interview, and nominate potential board members. The LIC can choose whomever they want from the entire membership without regard to geography, prior experience on the regional teams, or previous committee participation. Candidates submit curriculum vitae with an application, letter of intent, and written answers to questions posed by the LIC. Some or all of the applicants (depending on LIC interest in the candidate) are interviewed in person and a nomination is made. If more than one candidate is proposed, an election is held. But that's rarely happened, notes Albers.

Financial costs were key to reviewing current operations, as were survey results from regional team members who admitted they sometimes wondered why the positions existed and did not rate their own performance in the role highly. Further, volunteers identified their individual time pressures as challenging their ability to be effective for the association. Notes Albers, "When we first started talking about it, I was able to show, with specific costs, what the dollar investment of the regional teams was. I was able to demonstrate with data what [results] we got from these people, so we had the facts to back things up."

The association's bold move displaced volunteers from regional teams and committees, something organizations are usually loathe to do. The group took two steps to soften the blow. First, it agreed to review the decision several years in the future to determine if it was the right one. Second, it developed a Leadership Council for those who were moved out of their positions.

"We committed to looking at the change three or four years down the road," says Albers. But it was clear the change benefited the association and, consequently, there was no reason to return to previous operations.

The Leadership Council was another story. Though there was a job description for members of the council and they met at a social event at the annual conference every year, Albers notes, "It never really served any real significant purpose. Six or seven years later we got rid of it."

Changing governance isn't easy. But an effort to do so has more of a chance of succeeding when it is championed by volunteers, rather than staff, and is supported by factual data. Albers says, "Having a good, compelling, logical argument without getting into personality or emotional issues always wins the day"—an idea worth noting for radical change artists who also happen to be association executives.

CHAPTER THREE

Overhaul Committees

The traditional association governance structure includes a system of committees. Committees support the work of the board of directors either by handling responsibility for a specific association function or serving in a recommending capacity. In either case, they are more likely to be ineffective and unproductive than they are to be useful and constructive.

On paper, committees look great. They capture talent from the membership, focus this valuable resource on important association activities, and make a significant contribution in advancing the association's mission and objectives. Committee participation has several byproducts: It can engage members in a meaningful way, give members a networking opportunity, and provide the association with a pool of potential future leaders.

But let's face it, that's not how most committees work. If an association has a couple of active and productive committees, it is fortunate. There are associations or professional societies with active and worthwhile committee structures, but they are few and far between.

There are many reasons that committees don't work.

Based on our work with associations and years of interviewing volunteers, we estimate that at least 50 percent of committees don't have a clear understanding of what they are supposed to do. Rare is the board that will take time to think through what a committee's priority is or determine how to link their work to advance the goals and objectives in the strategic plan. Many committees spin their wheels for months on end trying to figure out what they are supposed to do. This is neither a great use of the valuable volunteer resource nor a positive experience for the committee chair or members.

Even when the board acknowledges that there isn't anything for a committee to undertake for the coming year, they will still appoint it and let it drift about for the year. They will say, "You never know, something might come up. We'll have them at the ready just in case." Again, this attitude does not foster good use of the valuable volunteer resource nor a positive experience for the committee chair or members.

In many instances, committees are formed by a "call for volunteers." Anybody who wants to can sign up for a committee. The motivators for board members mentioned previously (altruism, self interest, and ego) apply to committees as well. (In professional societies, more than a few simply want to add the committee to their résumés.) So 20 to 30 individuals on a committee have some interest in the area of the committee's responsibility and perhaps some knowledge or expertise in that area (or at least they think that they do). We start the year hoping that some competent members have signed up. Not a great beginning, but it gets worse. Most show up for the first meeting or conference call. Half way through the year, fewer than half are active. By the end of the year a handful are doing the work, and we hope that they are competent.

If you are lucky, one or two people on a committee will be truly productive. Sometimes an association board will acknowledge the fact that it really is just one person doing the work and they don't bother appointing anyone else.

In some instances, a committee will actually produce a well-thought-out recommendation and present it to the board. But all too often the board will reject, rework, or fail to act on the recommendation. In one association, an executive lamented about how the association failed to capitalize on committees that were actually doing good work. He said that the common response to a committee recommendation went like this:

"Thank you for your hard work. This recommendation is not exactly what we had in mind. And, quite frankly, we don't have the resources to fund anything in this area at this time." Again, this response is not a great use of the valuable volunteer resource or a positive experience for the committee chair or members.

Another scenario is when a committee chair hijacks a committee and runs it as a personal fiefdom, counter to the goals of the association. We've seen instances where an autocratic chair will run a committee for five to 10 years or more. No one dares challenge the despot. It is only until the program or activity becomes sadly and obviously obsolete that the decision is made to inject some new blood. In the meantime, the chair has driven off scores of volunteers whom the association will never see again because of their unpleasant and unproductive experiences.

Finally, committees may be populated with groupies with an interest in a particular area. They have no intention of doing any meaningful work, much less making recommendations. They just want an opportunity to meet and debate and network with peers who are knowledgeable or interested in an area of the profession or industry that is important to them. There is nothing wrong with this, but often they feel compelled to do something to demonstrate their value beyond the networking the committee offers. So they develop (or more likely have their staff liaison develop) some report to the board to justify their existence. Then they go back to their networking.

The reality is that staff usually does committee work. A long-time association professional recently commented: "It's getting towards the sunset of my career, so I don't have to play the game anymore. Let's quit the charade. 'The emperor has no clothes.' Volunteers on committees don't do much, if anything. The staff does it. So let's just call it what it is and stop wasting time kidding ourselves." The classic example of the charade of staff doing the committee's work is the budget or finance committee. When the chair is asked to make a report on the association's finances, he or she turns to the staff CFO or accountant and is handed the most recent financial statement.

The committee charade is costly. Staff sits back and watches as a time-pressed chair struggles to manage the committee and stay close to schedule. When the chair falls behind, the staff tries to step in but usually gets rebuffed the first time or two. Then when the situation gets hopelessly behind, the chair surrenders and staff comes in at the eleventh hour and gets the job done.

One final observation on committees: The system is almost always considered to be the source of future board members and officers. It is the farm team, the talent bank, the opportunity for members to demonstrate their abilities and for the association to monitor their performance. We have to ask: How can the traditional committee structure and dysfunction possibly produce the next generation of competent leaders? We believe that the majority of committees do not produce, do not capitalize on the volunteer resource at their disposal, do not result in a positive experience for the member, and in fact, drive off more members than they cultivate. And in many instances, the volunteers who survive are not always the best and the brightest. Though not always, they sometimes are groupies and wannabes who like to travel, hang with the big dogs, hobnob with peers, and feed their egos.

Radical Changes for Committees

The first radical change is that all committees or task forces are chaired by association staff professionals. In this role, they will be responsible for identifying, screening, qualifying, and selecting the right volunteers for the task. This helps ensure competence in the leadership of the committee and reduces the temptation to make appointments based on friendships and favors.

In this scenario, there are no more time-pressed, mostly ill-equipped volunteers running committees or task forces. We have to put responsibility for managing one of our most valuable and increasingly scarce resources—the volunteer member—in the hands of a professional. There will be considerable pushback to this move, primarily in the professional societies. Most involved volunteers in professional groups believe that only one of their own is capable of running a committee and that an outsider does not have the knowledge or understanding of the professional issues involved. (This is why they are more apt to hire chief staff executives from their profession; for example, many medical specialty executives are M.D.s.) In one instance, a volunteer decided against assigning a project to a staff person because she did "not possess the prerequisite professional ethos."

In the book, *Exposing the Elephants,* author Pamela Wilcox writes:

I'm the Expert is the conscious or unconscious belief that member, donor, or constituent expertise in occupation or cause (the benefit or mission of the organization) translates to expertise in nonprofit management (the business of the organization).The thinking goes like this: The American Bar Association (ABA) is about the law profession, so being a lawyer provides the necessary experience for managing an organization whose mission is law; the American Heart Association is about heart health, so being a volunteer who cares and is knowledgeable about heart-healthy activities provides the necessary expertise for managing an organization whose mission is heart health (page 26).

Wilcox identifies another aspect as well:

...many members, donors, and constituents believe that those who are not expert in the benefit component, professional staff, cannot possibly care about the organization as much as those who are experts, members, donors, and constituents. Furthermore, the underlying assumption is that unpaid (volunteers) are there because they care, but paid workers (professional staff) are there for the money (page 27).

Committee members can undoubtedly be the content experts. They bring invaluable expertise and insights. Managing the committee, however, requires a different set of skills. And possessing "professional ethos" is not one of them. You will see in our proposals for future association staff that their knowledge of the profession or industry will need to increase as a critical complement to their association management skills.

In our experience, volunteers in trade associations are more likely to empower and delegate to staff than their counterparts in the professional societies, who don't always recognize staff as executives with years of management experience. Leadership in trade associations are more likely to understand the importance of assigning the right work to the right people and ensuring the highest and best use of their human resources.

Managing volunteer committees or task forces takes skills that not everyone possesses. You must understand how to manage a project. You must understand how to communicate, build consensus, and deal with conflict. You have to know how to schedule and manage meetings. You must know how to make a recommendation and write a report and how to navigate the association's bureaucracy and work within its policies.

Some volunteers possess some of these skills. A few possess most of these skills. A rare number have all these skills. And some lack all of them.

Volunteer training and development programs can help, but often time-pressed members are unwilling to spend the time to participate. They want to get to the task at hand, prepared or not. And even if they do avail themselves of volunteer development opportunities, by the time they have had to practice them, the year has come and gone and another inexperienced member is in the driver's seat.

In addition to the skill set required to manage a committee or task force is the fact that the issues we now ask committees and task forces to address are more complex. They aren't simple tasks. They require a higher level of sophistication than in the past. And a part-time amateur (also known as a volunteer) is often out of his or her depth.

A good example here is meeting site selection and hotel contract negotiations. In the good old days a committee handled these functions. They went on site selection trips and had a hands-on role in making the meeting arrangements. Today the legal complexities of contracts and room blocks as well as the intricacies of negotiating arrangements are considerable—not necessarily something you want to leave to a practicing CPA or dental hygienist.

Another example would be state lobbying for a profession. Decades ago, a committee of a handful of doctors with an understanding of and interest in the political process could handle the job for a state medical society. In recent years, this has been out of the question. A professional lobbyist is required.

Putting professional staff in charge of managing committees has consequences for staff competencies and qualifications. Staff must know the industry or profession at a level many association staff have not had to in the past. They don't have to have industry or profession experience (although they might) but they must have a basic, well-grounded under-standing of the profession or industry. In many cases, this will require significantly upgrading staff whose only role in the past was to "hang the coats and take the notes."

Once professional staff is in the driver's seat, they will have the authority to put together their committee or task force. And like board composition, the process to do so must be based on the competencies needed to get the job done. Not who knows who. Not who wants to. But instead, what does the committee need in terms of talent and knowledge? Which members (or nonmembers) could bring that to the table? Of those that could, who are the three to five individuals best qualified?

Professional staff will need to be a little like search consultants, using search-like processes to identify and recruit the right players for the team. They might have a database of members organized by expertise and experience. They will know how to seek out and qualify candidates. And once a committee is assembled, they will have to know how to manage the people and the process in a way that makes the highest and best use of the volunteer resources at hand.

An association executive described the approach as "Just in Time (JIT)" volunteer utilization. In JIT manufacturing, parts arrive only as needed. You don't have inventory sitting around idly. And in this approach by associations, you don't have volunteers sitting around idly. You don't mobilize them until you need them. And when you need them, you use a rigorous identification and selection process to optimize results.

The net result is a significant improvement in the quality of engagement for the volunteer. Research has identified engagement as an important key to affiliation. But it is folly to believe that any and all committee engagement is positive and results in a stronger tie to the association. One could argue that much of the current committee experience is marginally satisfying or meaningful, and some of it is frankly negative and disappointing. The time-pressed environment raises the expectations of those considering committee service. A volunteer with an unsatisfactory committee experience is likely to go back to work, family, and friends and let other members spin their wheels on the association's committees.

As you assess how to overhaul committees, the following guidelines will help:

Decide how many committees you really need. Before redesigning the way your committees function, conduct a zero-based assessment of the current committees. Analyze their performance and contributions. Sunset the marginal groups. It makes no sense to redesign a committee that you don't need and is not a good use of your resources.

Get the facts to make your case. In the process of this assessment, develop data on committee performance. Know where your committees are producing and where they do not perform. You will need specific instances of where committees have floundered, where committee chairs have dropped the ball, where deadlines have been missed, where budgets have been overrun, where staff has had to come to the rescue at the eleventh hour. Naming volunteers who haven't performed has its risks, so work with a small core of volunteer leaders in presenting this evaluation to minimize political fallout, and keep the list close to your vest. You are likely to find that more volunteers than you expect see the failings of the current system.

Clearly define the role of the committee chair and the skills required to do the job. Document the functions expected from a committee chair regardless of the type or charge of the committee. Determine if some committees have different roles than others. Then list the skills or abilities that are necessary to execute these responsibilities. The same goes for task forces or ad hoc groups.

Determine the committee situations where the knowledge or expertise is available only through a member. Document the circumstances where only a member can provide the input or content required to get the job done. Then list where member input might be helpful but not critical. This will provide a valuable guide in making sure that the volunteer resource is optimized and focused on meaningful work.

Identify the individuals who will stand in the way. As with board downsizing, list the involved volunteers who are likely to oppose the change. The most likely are long-time chairpersons. Upcoming volunteers with an eye on a chair position are another. Make a list, understand their argument for the status quo, and be prepared to respond.

Focus the conversion on a few committees as a start. You may not be able to convert the entire committee structure to this model. Identify committees where you have the strongest argument for staff management and where your staff is currently effective and respected. The easiest to select are those committees that do not have a significant need for member knowledge or expertise. Pick committees that you know performance improvement will be obvious and come quickly.

Demonstrate results. Present the board with the results. Show how projects or tasks have been accomplished more quickly than in the past. Show how volunteer resources were optimized. Show how the outcomes were superior to those of the traditional system. Emphasize the value of the synergy of staff and volunteers working together, side-by-side, rather than in the traditional "us versus them" mentality that often occurs in associations between staff and volunteers.

Convert additional committees as you are able. Once you've demonstrated results, you'll likely find volunteer support for streamlined committees that do valuable and relevant work. As the volunteer experience becomes more meaningful and the sense of accomplishment increases for those involved, you may gain the support you need to convert most, if not all, of your committees. Doing so requires entrusting staff with more responsibility than ever before. Not only does the concept ensure that volunteers are spending time doing meaningful work rather than simply rubber-stamping decisions, it also gives the association the opportunity to challenge staff and help ensure they are working up to their full potential. This makes it easier to recruit and retain top performers, a topic we'll address in the next chapter as we discuss the importance of empowering both the CEO and staff.

CHAPTER FOUR

Empower the CEO and Enhance Staff

The first dividend of the five-member, competency-based board will be the empowerment of a heretofore vastly underutilized chief executive and staff.

The CEO now has a board that is an asset versus one that may have been a ball and chain: five carefully selected leaders from the profession or industry, each with governance experience, and each possessing a competency strategically matched with the association's priorities and direction. And this board is supported by staff-chaired committees that are focused and aligned with the association's priorities.

Several strong trends have been driving the transition to staff empowerment and these trends will continue to contribute to growing the delegation of responsibility to staff.

First, the time pressures on volunteer leaders are placing significant limitations on their ability to contribute to the association as in the past. As we noted earlier, volunteers are busier than ever before because of a variety of factors. The result is diminished time for association work. And when they do have time, it is compromised by personal and professional distractions and interruptions. All you have to do is observe a board meeting today. Directors come late and leave early. They jump out of the meeting room for phone calls. They email and text during board deliberations. So even when the association gets their time, the quality attention and effort required is lacking.

Further, associations and professional societies have become complex organizations. They have considerably expanded their scope of programs, services, and activities (often to their detriment, as we shall see in Chapter Six). Their information systems are more sophisticated than ever. Their communications vehicles are multifaceted. Their organizational relationships have expanded. Their financial and legal structures are more complicated. All these factors result in the need for increased management competencies and the need to delegate responsibilities previously handled by volunteers to staff professionals.

Volunteers have an extremely wide range of skills, abilities, and experiences. But they are not professional association executives. When it comes to running an association, that makes them amateurs, or "persons inexperienced or unskilled in a particular activity," as the dictionary defines it.

Further, though board members have varying levels of commitment to their association, from modest to considerable, they are not full-time executives.

The association or professional society of the future cannot be run by part-time amateurs. But it can be run by a five-member board and an empowered and skill-enhanced staff.

The new five-person governance structure will unleash the potential of association staff as never before. And it will make the highest and best use of the volunteer resource as well. Gone are the misguided agendas of well-intentioned but disconnected volunteers. Gone are the countless delays in decision making. Gone are the missed opportunities resulting from cumbersome approval processes. Gone are the innumerable hours of committee members' spinning their wheels. Instead of slow and lumbering, the association will be streamlined and lean.

If you believe that this is naively optimistic, look no farther than the functioning of Executive Committees. We think you will agree that for the most part, they work quite well. Officers are far more engaged than members of a large board. The dynamics of the small group are far more productive than a large board. And with the exception of a little micromanaging here and there, they stay focused on important governance issues. Remember, this five-member competency-based board has been carefully vetted and selected. The members understand their role and the importance of optimizing the association's human resources.

Similarly, an empowered CEO and staff also understand their roles and the importance of optimizing the association's resources. With this in mind, let's take a look at how a "new and improved" association operates.

A professional society retained an outside consultant for assistance with planning the annual conference, the society's primary meeting with a significant educational component. The society had a meeting planner on staff and had previously developed the conference internally. The consultant was retained with the belief that outside expertise would strengthen the conference's performance and value.

The Education Committee, responsible for determining the educational content and selecting the presenters, had completed its work and their recommendations had been approved. All educational topics and speakers had been finalized.

The consultant was engaged to assist the society with the format and organization of the conference components: general sessions, educational tracks, workshops, and social events.

The process began with requests for proposals developed by staff, reviewed by the president and president-elect, and distributed to 10 potential consultants. The incoming proposals were reviewed by the president, president-elect, CEO, and the director of meetings. This same group of four interviewed three finalists and selected the consultant, then participated in a series of conference calls with the consultant. After clarifying the objectives and determining the schedule, the consultant developed a series of drafts of a design for the conference for review and feedback. This involved four hour-long conference calls to achieve agreement on the final approved conference format.

The process required the following of the president, president-elect, CEO, and the director of meetings:

Action	Hours	Cost at $200/hour
Review of RFP draft	4	$800
Feedback on RFP draft	4	$800
Review of 2nd draft	4	$800
Feedback on 2nd draft	4	$800
Approval of RFP	4	$800
Review of proposals	8	$1,600
Selection of finalists	8	$1,600
Interviews of finalist	32	$6,400
Project initiation call with consultant	4	$800
Review of 4 conference design drafts	16	$3,200
Conference calls for draft feedback	16	$3,200
Total	**104**	**$20,800**

The estimates of time required are conservative. It does not include staff time to develop the initial RFP. It does not include the time to set up the conference calls. It does not include the intangible time spent thinking about the project while in the shower or on the commute to work. The rate of $200 per hour is also conservative.

This society spent well over $20,000 and more than 100 hours on this project. A case could be made that it was as much as $40,000, depending on the actual cost per hour.

Commentary

- This traditional approach was a gross misuse of the society's most valuable resource: its human capital. It allocated its most valuable volunteer resources on work that could have been handled almost in its entirety by the director of meetings in a fraction of the time rather than asking high-level volunteers to focus on more challenging issues facing the association.

- It is highly unlikely that anyone estimated or tracked the time required or the cost to the society.

- The president and president-elect felt very good about the progress being made and the concrete results being achieved. Managing a tangible project is far easier than making decisions about priorities or direction. But the volunteers' time would have been better spent wrestling with issues facing the membership as a whole rather than developing a new educational approach.

- The CEO went along with the leadership. If that's what they wanted to spend their time on, OK. But it would be unwise to not be involved. Unattended and without guidance, volunteer leaders may make well-intentioned but flawed decisions.

- The conference work that required the knowledge and insights of the society's professionals had already been appropriately tapped by the Education Committee's developing the educational content and recommending presenters for the conference.

- The president and president-elect were not likely to add any substantive value to the ideas in the drafting process or in the ultimate decision making, other than to inject their personal preferences and biases.

- The CEO's involvement in the details of the conference format should have been delegated to the director of meetings.

- The opportunity cost of allocating hours of time and energy by the president, president-elect, and CEO to this effort were considerable. What if they had spent that valuable time addressing a professional issue or trend and analyzing its impact on the society? What if they had spent the same time considering opportunities for the society to capitalize on internet technology? What if they had assessed potential partnering possibilities with related organizations or other stakeholders?

- In an association with an empowered CEO and staff with the ability to hire expertise as needed, the director of meetings would be charged with retaining a consultant approved by the CEO. The director of meetings would work with the consultant to develop a recommended format for approval by the CEO. The CEO would inform the president and president-elect of the new conference design.

As you can see, there's a huge difference between how the old model works and how the new could work when it comes to speed and efficiency. Even more important, the new model more fully capitalizes on human potential—both staff and volunteer—in a way that allows the two to partner according to their strengths. Staff gets the room and permission they need to respond to the needs of the association and its members, while volunteers contribute according to their experience and expertise. Synergy is unleashed. New partnerships emerge. Energy increases. And the association is revitalized.

Candor Is Key

Another benefit of the new governance model is that it encourages honest communication and straightforwardness between staff and volunteers. With fewer players, trust can be built more quickly and dissension identified more readily. The smaller circle of leadership requires a new level of teamwork; there's no room for lack of commitment or avoidance of accountability, two dysfunctions identified by Patrick Lencioni in his book, *The Five Dysfunctions of a Team.*

The traditional association model is often corrupted by a lack of candor. Staff regularly credits board members or committee chairs with accomplishments with which they had little to do. Or volunteers simply take credit for staff work. Staff stands by in silence while volunteers make inaccurate statements or misrepresent situations. Officers can be reluctant to confront the CEO over an issue, preferring to let it slide. In particular, the chief staff executive's annual performance appraisal is regularly postponed or skipped. Board members don't deal with each other frankly, preferring to "go along to get along." The system is often rife with fraud.

Such lack of honesty results in volunteers and staff operating in an environment that can be far from reality. Some associations have been going through the charade for so long they begin to accept it as reality.

Leaner governance encourages candor because staff and volunteers have a clearer picture of what each should be doing. In the best case, the two groups are working together as a tightly knit team in an environment that invites spirited discussion and intense debate followed by clear consensus. In this atmosphere, each group can do its best work.

Roles and Responsibilities by the Book

While the change in governance structure allows for better use of staff and volunteer time with more candor between the two groups, some things remain the same, including the roles and responsibilities of the board and staff, which have been documented countless times in association publications.

In general, the board is responsible for governing the association by setting broad policies and objectives; retaining the CEO; ensuring that the association has adequate resources; and guiding the association in the best interests of its members.

The CEO is responsible for running the association in a way that meets the objectives established by the board. The executive is responsible for decisions about what is to be done, how it is to be done, and who is to do it.

While there are variations in the way roles and responsibilities are codified, they have been essentially consistent for decades. But in spite of thousands of board development sessions, hundreds of articles, and scores of books on the subject, volunteer leaders continue to inject themselves inappropriately into management decisions and operations in all but the most disciplined organizations.

Why? The answer is simple. It is easier to manage than to govern. Though most volunteers have experience in managing, they have much less time in a governing role. Further, much of managing is independent decision making, often on short-term immediate issues, while governance requires consensus on bigger-picture issues. Not all managers have been trained in the art of reaching consensus. Finally, much of managing is black and white, while governance is grey because governance decisions require someone to consider multiple constituencies. People naturally gravitate to what is easier, which is what pushes people from governance to managing roles. Volunteers are constantly "off sides" even in the best of circumstances. It is time to acknowledge that trying to fix the "govern versus manage" conundrum is futile. That is one reason why the small, competency-based board is essential: to eradicate the costly and misguided malpractice of large, poorly constituted boards.

Though misguided volunteers can be a challenge, there are many situations where the chief executive and other staff are part of the problem. They are understandably reluctant to challenge volunteers when they cross the line because they don't want to damage relationships or risk their jobs. Why challenge a micromanaging committee chair? Why challenge a board member involved in a matter more appropriately handled by staff? When job security is the objective, capitulation to rogue volunteers is an understandably tempting course to take.

Does a carefully selected small board ensure eradication of volunteers doing what should be done by staff? Will it eliminate volunteer micromanagement? Probably not. The temptation to slide from governance to management will always be there. Managing is more tangible, with outcomes or resulting feedback often immediate. The politics involved in governing are intricate. Governing decisions are more difficult than management decisions. But the costly consequences of "off sides" volunteers and enabling staff will be significantly reduced and the volunteer and staff resource optimized as never before if new models are followed.

The Mindset Regarding Staff

The thinking that underlies the board/staff relationship varies from association to association and from board to board. The mindset is largely a function of three things: association culture, the personalities of both staff and volunteers, and history. We'll start with history.

Boards are reactionary. If an executive from the profession or industry previously failed, the response is often to hire an association professional. If an association professional failed, there can be a point of view that the next executive must come from the profession or industry. The thinking is that only someone with a background and hands-on experience in the industry is capable of running the association. (In some cases, an executive from the profession is even required in the bylaws.) If a hire from inside failed, the response is to go outside for the successor. If a strong executive failed, the response is to find an administrator. One can only hope that this is not the only criteria and that management skills required for a tax-exempt membership organization are considered as well.

The mindset regarding staff can be additionally challenging when there is a culture of staff servitude. In this case, volunteer leaders are masters and staffers are vassals. This is an unfortunate situation but it still exists. There is an arrogant attitude among some "leaders" that volunteers are the only enlightened ones in the structure and that staff's ability is limited to administrative or low-level responsibilities. Sometimes there is an organization-wide superiority complex, in other situations it is an attitude held only by some individuals. This governance mentality guarantees that the staff resource is underutilized. And consider the impact of this "leadership" style on the ability of the association to attract and retain a quality workforce. Who would want to work there?

Another component of the mindset often is, "This organization is ours and we need to run it." We hear the old saw repeated to association executives over and over again: "Don't forget: It is not your association." In addition to volunteers waving this flag, executives often remind one another of this same thing, purportedly to keep each other out of hot water.

We don't get this thinking. Do CEOs in corporate America remind each other that the corporations do not belong to them? Do they need to be reminded that the stockholders own the company? Do we not want our association executives to be stewards, to be passionate and committed, to run the association as if it is their own? Or do we prefer our staff to be bureaucrats who couldn't care less about the organization because it's "not theirs"? While staff does not have the legal right of possession, we would certainly want them to act as if they did.

When volunteers cross the line into management activities, an underlying assumption is that anybody can run an association. Any optometrist, any distributor, any librarian, any engineer. This assumption is made from limited exposure to what it really takes and an incomplete understanding of what is entailed. But it looks easy. How difficult could it be to run an association department? The CEO position looks particularly easy. Executives travel to meetings, often in luxurious resort locations. They attend social events and go to lavish dinners. They don't have the pressure of producing a bottom line. They have nice offices and plenty of support staff. Most anybody could handle that, right? Wrong.

The Skill Set of the Future

Not only does today's association require more than full-time management; new competencies are also necessary. Some of these are just now emerging; others have yet to be identified. As demands increase, it becomes even less likely that volunteers can adequately fit the bill. For example, in 2009 the CFA Institute hired a director of innovation and emerging media. This individual's charge is to use social media to raise the profile of the association's credential, listen to constituents online, create communities to help enhance member loyalty and affinity for CFA, and drive members and potential members to the organization's online portal.

Can you imagine volunteers doing this effectively for the association?

Instead of expecting part-time volunteers to possess the necessary skill and expertise, smart leaders will increasingly look to staff. As a result, successful chief staff executives and staff specialists will need to acquire an increased level of industry or professional expertise. As they assume more responsibility, they will need an in-depth understanding of how the industry or profession functions, how the players interact, the dynamics of the marketplace, competitive and strategic factors, and technical trends and their implications.

In the old model, staff brought functional skills to complement the industry or professional expertise of volunteers. Communications professionals processed volunteer content into publications. Meetings professionals packaged volunteer knowledge into conferences. Staff harnessed volunteer expertise into standards or certification programs. But with diminished volunteer resources, staff will be required to fill the gap.

In the old model, when an inquiry came into the office, it would be channeled to the appropriate staff who would say, "I'll find an answer somewhere and get right back to you." The staff of the future will more likely be capable of providing the solution directly.

CEOs will no longer make a seamless change from one industry or profession to another. No longer will an association communications manager easily transition from a manufacturing association to a medical society or an education director switch from one profession to another. The key management positions will continue to require the functional skills, but the requirement for industry or professional knowledge will increase significantly.

This will add fuel to the ongoing debate: Does the association hire someone from the profession or industry or an association professional? For the most part, the association community recoils at the suggestion of the former because it implies that association management is not a real profession and that anybody can do it. But regardless of which route an association goes, the executive from the industry or profession will have to quickly acquire association management competencies, and the association professional will have to quickly gain industry or professional knowledge.

The Staff Quality Dividend

One unmentioned benefit of a competency-based board is its attractiveness to potential CEOs. What top-notch association executive would not be interested in working with this governance model? What outstanding association executive would not consider trading the current board structure for a small, carefully selected competency-based board of leaders?

When you take into account the impact of subsequent radical changes we propose that will invigorate and revitalize the association, think of the repositioned association's ability to attract quality staff. Today's association model is mature at best, more likely in decline. Where do people want to work: in an organization that is tired and struggling or in an organization with energy and strategy? Sears or Amazon? The U.S. Postal Service or FedEx? *Chicago Tribune* or Google?

High-quality staff not only will be topic experts but also will be skilled in bringing out the best in volunteers. As the old adage says, "Iron sharpens iron." As volunteers expect more from staff, staff will rise to the occasion. And as they rise to the occasion, they'll take volunteers with them. As a result, the entire team will become stronger and more effective.

Current Trend

The delegation of work to staff sorely lags behind the challenges confronting associations. The price of volunteers hanging on to roles for which they lack necessary skills and adequate time in today's association is costly. It results in poor decision making, delayed action, suboptimization of staff, and missed opportunities. This lag in appropriately empowering staff is most painfully evident in associations' inadequate adoption of technology, which we will address in Chapter Seven.

There is tangible evidence that associations are moving in the direction of empowered staffs, but it is taking far too long. An examination of titles for the CEO shows that more of these positions are now president and/or chief executive officer versus the executive director of recent years or the executive secretary from earlier days. Of the 953 organizations responding to the ASAE "Association Compensation and Benefits Study, 2008–2009 Edition," some 46 percent use the chief executive officer or president title or a combination thereof. While the move toward changing titles is a manifestation of the board's transferring authority to the chief staff executive, a change in thinking must accompany the change in terminology. A president that is still treated as an executive secretary is an executive secretary. The trend clearly shows the direction of associations, but it also shows that the transition is slow and many associations cling to the old model, as 54 percent of those organizations responding to the benefits survey still use a traditional title.

Next, the compensation of association executives and staff indicates an increased appreciation for the growing need to acquire the professional expertise required to operate an association in today's environment. The median total compensation for chief executive officers increased 6.3 percent between 2008 and 2010, according to ASAE's *2010 Compensation and Benefits Study.* Increases for other staff positions ranged from a low of 1 percent to a high of 19.3 percent.

And finally, the average size of an association staff has grown. As associations have expanded and become more complex organizations, volunteers are incapable of making the contributions necessary. The required skills and expertise simply do not exist in the volunteer base. They must be hired or outsourced and it appears that more associations are doing this. Compare the average number of full-time staff equivalents of 23, according to ASAE's *1996 Policies and Procedures,* with the average of 35 (reported in the 2006 version of the same report—an increase of 34 percent in just 10 years). The trend is toward staff growth.

A Caution

As we look at the issue of empowered staff, we need to note that all current staff are not going to fit, a thought that may be unpopular. Some staff will be incapable of assuming additional responsibility. Some will not be able to acquire the level of professional or industry knowledge required. In many cases, staff are not performing adequately in their current roles, lacking contemporary skills. The change to an empowered staff will magnify the mismatch of staff who have not maintained necessary skills with the new challenges for staff in an empowered environment. Taking an honest assessment of staff will be necessary and making changes as a result will be difficult. But the reward is worth it. As Jim Collins writes in *Good to Great:*

> The executives who ignited the transformation from good to great did not first figure out where to drive the bus and then get people to take it there. No they *first* got the right people on the bus (and the wrong people off the bus) and *then* figured out where to drive it.
>
> The good-to-great leaders understood three simple truths. First, if you begin with "who," rather than "what," you can more easily adapt to a changing world.... Second, if you have the right people on the bus, the problem of how to motivate and manage people largely goes away. The right people don't need to be tightly managed or fired up; they will be self-motivated by the inner drive to produce the best result and to be part of creating something great. Third, if you have the wrong people, it doesn't matter whether you discover the right direction; you *still* won't have a great company (pages 41-42).

Implementation

The following steps are designed to support the empowered staff model and encourage improved candor in the volunteer-staff relationship:

Institute a three-year strategic planning cycle. Commit to a three-year strategic planning cycle with the board and key staff as equal participants. This should be designed to build consensus on the association's direction, priorities, and most importantly, resource concentration. "This is nothing new," you say. Yet a 1986 Lawrence-Leiter survey found that 38 percent of associations operated without a strategic plan, and we doubt that this has changed much in the last 25 years.

Conduct an annual performance appraisal of the CEO. The board must discipline itself to complete a thorough and thoughtful performance appraisal of the chief staff executive. The performance measurements for objectives in the strategic and technology plans (outlined in Chapter Seven) should be an integral component of the evaluation. The timing of the evaluation should be scheduled annually and aligned with the annual board self-evaluation.

Complete an annual board self-evaluation process. The board should commit to an annual self-evaluation process, including an annual survey and action plan. The timing should be consistent with the performance evaluation of the CEO, and the performance measurements for objectives in the strategic and technology plans (which we address in Chapter Seven) should also be an integral component of this self-evaluation. To foster a candid environment, the responses should be attributed to each participant and not be confidential.

Perform evaluation and feedback surveys after each board meeting. The board and key staff should complete a brief evaluation and feedback survey following each board meeting. This should be short, requiring no more than three to five minutes to complete. It is probably best to distribute and collect this one-page questionnaire at the conclusion of the meeting. The survey instrument should include performance ratings on key elements of the meeting and provide an opportunity for feedback to improve the productivity of future meetings.

Though the above aren't earth-shattering suggestions, we're surprised by how many boards don't regularly plan, provide feedback for their top executive, or evaluate themselves and how they are working as a team. Though each step individually is small, together they will provide enormous dividends. And, as you move to competency-based boards, they are an essential part of ensuring effective communication and smooth operations. Finally, with the foundation outlined above, it's easier to complete the tasks outlined in the next chapter, which calls for a careful look at identifying who you'll serve as your member market.

Radical Change: Rethinking Staff Expertise

ASSOCIATION: Electrical Apparatus Service Association (EASA)

BUDGET: $2.6 million

NUMBER OF STAFF MEMBERS: 16

NUMBER OF MEMBERS: 1,950

CASE STUDY:

Does your association offer a member service that's so valuable it ties your members to you? The Electrical Apparatus Service Association's (EASA's) answer desk, designed to provide technical support to members repairing motors and other electromechanical equipment, is one of its most highly valued services—so valued, in fact, that the association just hired its fourth engineer to handle the call volume that continues to increase each year. This new engineer expands the association's focus to pump and vibration analysis in addition to its core competency of electric motor and generator repair. Currently, staff engineers respond to 50 to 100 calls per day.

The association's members sell and repair electric motors, pumps, controls, wind generators, and other electromechanical equipment. While members sell new equipment when that is the best solution for the customer, often a replacement is not available or economically viable, so repair is the best option—and that's where the EASA's answer desk offers value to members. Staff engineers consult with members encountering a problem when working on a job either in their service center or in the field. Members call the association for assistance and usually are able to troubleshoot with an engineer within an hour. "We have engineers on staff who can help with electric motor redesign, process questions, application questions, and how-to questions, including pump and vibration analysis issues," says Linda Raynes, president & CEO. "Because of this, our resonance and value to members has increased over the last 12 years."

It appears that the value will only continue to increase because of changes in the market, says Raynes. "We believe that part of the reason that we're getting more and more phone calls, and will continue to do so, is that there is really no education in the college systems for the blue collar but technical work of electromechanical repair and rewinding.... You have fewer people and a lot of the expertise is retiring, so you naturally have more people who are going to call in and ask questions when they have a piece of equipment they have not dealt with previously."

Fewer people in the field and a workforce that's retiring have provided both an opportunity and a challenge for the association. More members need the technical assistance offered by the answer desk but the increasing number of retirements makes it difficult to find adequately trained engineers to staff it. The best staffers have both experience in the field and an understanding of the theory behind the equipment. Raynes notes, "If you have experienced some of the same challenges as the member that's calling, you can certainly help them a lot more, if nothing else, with more empathy, but also it's that direct repair and application experience that makes a difference."

The required mix of theory and experience is a delicate balance—so much so that the association has developed its own method of testing to determine both theory and design knowledge when hiring call center staff. It's a step Raynes advocates for other associations considering developing in-house technical support. But first, an association must clearly understand member needs. "Initially, I would encourage others to do a really extensive market study of their membership to determine just what type of service they need." Hiring is easier when you know exactly what expertise you are looking for.

EASA carries liability insurance in case errant information is offered and uses disclaimers to remind members that information is provided in good faith but ultimately, the member is responsible. To date, the association hasn't had to use the insurance and though staffing the answer desk can be a challenge, Raynes notes that member needs assessment surveys repeatedly show that access to staff engineers is highest on the list. "If there's anything in the association world anymore called a golden handcuff, that's what this is for us," she says.

Radical Change: Independent Contractors Add to Staff Expertise

ASSOCIATION: Ohio Society of Certified Public Accountants

BUDGET: $10 million

NUMBER OF STAFF MEMBERS: 49

NUMBER OF MEMBERS: 23,000

CASE STUDY:

There was no such thing as the internet when Clarke Price, CAE, started working for the Ohio Society of Certified Public Accountants (OSCPA). Yet he's harnessed its power to develop what's become one of the strongest retention tools for the society: an independent contractor who provides answers for member tax accountants via an online forum. The addition recognizes the value of staffing to provide direct solutions and answers to members, whether by captive staff or independent contractors.

Like many organizations, the OSCPA developed a listserver for members in the early days of the internet. Members used it to ask one another for input regarding tax questions. Though the exchange was valuable, the information shared wasn't always accurate. That's when Price's team saw an opportunity. They thought, "Let's get somebody who can give an authoritative answer." In this case, the desire for member access to expertise led to a new member service. Though expertise wasn't available on staff, Price was empowered to find it. The service has been so successful for the Tax Section that the society is introducing it now to its Accounting and Auditing Sections.

Though members pay an additional fee to be a member of a section, the fee is nominal (between $25 and $45). In addition to access to the independent contractor providing tax answers, section members receive electronic newsletters with news specific to their areas of interest. Rather than adding to staff, however, a former employee is now on contract to provide information for the newsletter, and a respected tax educator (also an independent contractor) provides answers to the questions members ask.

The value provided by the answer service is enhanced by its specificity. Notes Price, "When we answer, we try to point members in the right direction. Where there's a code section citation we can provide, we provide it, such as 'Internal Revenue Service Code Section 7216' or whatever we can provide so that it's not a blind hunt for members." The assistance is especially valuable to sole practitioners, those in small firms, and those who work in isolation in a larger company (e.g., a CPA's working as a controller or chief financial officer). "What we hear from our constituency is that we provide great value through these expert resources," says Price. They say, "It gives me that resource I need to get a quick answer so I can come across intelligently where I work."

"Clearly, this has made a difference in retention because members attach value for what they get from the sections," says Price. "Looking at the retention trend, it's clearly positive."

The keys to the society's success are numerous. First, OSCPA recognized the value of providing access to expertise as a solid member service rather than one supported only as staff is able. Second, based on its early experience with the listservers, the society knew what members wanted. Price suggests, "Make sure you've got a structure that makes sense. Focus on the key issues where members are looking for information. Do some research, whether it is formal or informal, about what the members want."

Price advises other association executives to constantly question. "A major portion of my job is to identify issues and ask, 'What about this?' or 'Is there something in this that represents an opportunity or threat for us? And how do we respond?'" Further, as his staff considers possible new services, he notes that they recognize the "need to give information context. We need to leverage the information and help our members understand and process it. That's a very valuable jumping off point."

What information should you be leveraging, processing, and providing context to for your members? By asking and answering the questions above, you will also have a jumping off point—one that may produce a highly valued member service for your association as well.

CHAPTER FIVE

Rationalize the Member Market

The Realities of Today's Member Market

For 50 years, industry consolidation and professional specialization trends have resulted in an unprecedented quandary for most associations: How do we serve an increasingly diverse member market? How do we serve a member market that has changed significantly from the one that the association was designed for?

In the past, the typical association's approach was to focus on members' considerable common interests and needs. Now common interests and needs are scarce. As a matter of fact, the interests of one member are sometimes diametrically opposed to those of another member. What is an association to do?

When you boil it all down, there are only three options: (A) continue to struggle with divergent interests and needs; (B) organize and structure to meet diverse needs; or (C) focus solely on the needs of a definable segment.

The first option is not defensible. For an association's governance and management to acknowledge the situation and its consequences but do nothing would represent a major failure in their obligations. This would be like a newspaper seeing the impact of digital information alternatives and saying they're not going to do anything differently. "Let's ignore this and keep doing what we have always done."

The second option has been tried but with marginal success in most cases. Ask any association with sections, special interest groups or divisions, "How are they working?" and the answer will be "It varies. A few work well, some do OK, and others do poorly." There are several reasons. First, running special interests groups are typically not the priority of the association: providing core services is. Plus, special interest groups are insufficiently supported with staff, which means that they are heavily dependent on volunteers. Management by well-intentioned but time-pressed volunteers often results in low quality deliverables offered sporadically.

Obviously, the last option—focusing on the needs of a definable segment—is the radical course we recommend.

Despite marginal success, special interest groups, sections, and divisions within associations have grown rapidly. For example, recognizing the wide variety of its members, the National Speakers Association introduced "Professional Expert Groups" designed to create smaller groups of like-minded individuals within the association. Groups include those for humorists, keynoters, seminar leaders, facilitators, and business coaches. These special interests groups are designed to address the disparate needs of an increasingly complex and diverse member market.

But sections and special interest groups all have one thing in common: They cling to the member market as traditionally defined. No one says, "You know what? We can't serve all these diverse segments. Let's rethink the fundamental scope of a member market that we can serve well and purposefully forget about those member segments where we will always have marginal value." No one says, "The market and the players in it have changed to the extent that we are attempting to serve a member market that doesn't exist anymore."

The days of homogenous markets are long gone. And they will never return at the scale that they once existed. Consequently, the days of the broad-based association's or professional society's ability to add value to diverse and complex member markets is coming to an end. Does focusing solely on the needs of a definable segment mean yours will be a smaller association? It might. If it looks that way, ask yourself: "Would our members want to belong to a large association or an association that helps them perform and succeed?" We don't think members give a lot of thought to the size of an association versus the value they receive.

Industry consolidation and globalization have rendered many trade association's traditional member markets virtually unserviceable. The typical trade association can no longer serve all automobile dealers, or manufacturers, or contractors. The bimodal distribution of companies in a consolidated industry results in segments with so little in common that they are unserviceable in any meaningful and economically compelling way. The typical result of a consolidated industry is a limited number of very large companies which represent a high share of total industry sales on one end and at the other end a larger number of small companies that are usually specialists or niche players. These two segments have very little in common. The large companies have little need for many services traditionally provided by the association. On the other hand, the small companies need the very services that the large companies don't, including the collective buying power of a group that an association can provide.

Differing needs often results in conflict. In 2009, Pacific Gas and Electric, PNM Resources, and Exelon dropped membership in the U.S. Chamber of Commerce and Nike resigned its seat on the Chamber board over its climate change positions. The Associated General Contractors (AGC) and its affiliated chapters strain to grow membership as companies in the construction industry morph into new organizational configurations and business models, with many traditional members not even calling themselves "general contractors" any more. Many today have become "construction managers" and their companies are structured and operated very differently from their predecessor general contractors. The member market for the American Forest and Paper Association (AFPA) has changed dramatically, resulting in industry segments with competing interests and agendas. AFPA's members used to own both the timberland and the processes of production of fiber into paper and wood products. Now timberland is owned separately from paper and wood production. Owners of timberland want high prices for their product; paper and wood producers want low-cost raw materials. AFPA has responded with a strategy to focus on the wood and paper products segment of the industry. As noted previously, specialization (often combined with industry consolidation) has a similar impact on professional societies. The broad-based professional society can no longer serve all physicians, or certified public accountants, or engineers. The diversity of practice in almost all professions results in multiple constituencies with less and less in common.

The American Medical Association (AMA) and its constituent state and local societies have been unable to serve a population of doctors who are increasingly diverse in practices and interests. Hand surgeons don't need the same information as family practitioners. Hospital-based physicians require different advocacy than rural, solo practitioners. And plastic surgeons have little, if anything, in common with pediatricians. Similarly, the American Bar Association's (ABA's) membership is declining, while the number of attorneys in the United States is growing at 1 to 2 percent a year. The American Institute of CPAs is confronted with a trend that results in 50 percent of CPAs who do not work in the traditional areas of public tax and audit practice.

Emergence of Specialty Associations

The downside of a broad-based association and the advantages of an association focused on a tightly defined member market have resulted in the rapid growth of specialty trade associations and professional societies. Though we may not have noticed, the market has been telling us something through the emergence of these groups with more narrowly defined members.

The U.S. manufacturing industry spawned scores of trade associations from 1930 to 1950 as companies gravitated to trade associations focused on their particular segment of manufacturing. Attorneys have joined associations focused solely on their specific area of practice: trial law, criminal defense, family law, district attorneys, and others.

The most dramatic demonstration of the potential of the single focus association is in medicine. While the American Medical Association's membership and market share have plummeted, the number of specialty and subspecialty medical societies has grown. The American Board of

Medical Specialties certifies physicians in more than 145 specialties and subspecialties. With an average estimated membership of 5,300 in a specialty organization (according to Rebecca Brandt, CAE, executive director, American Association of Medical Society Executives), more than 768,500 physicians could be members of these groups (the estimate does not account for cross-over memberships of physicians), compared to the AMA's membership, which *MedPage Today* (June 12, 2006) estimated "only represents 135,300 'real, practicing physicians' as of 2005."

A review of the growth of associations over the last 50 years shows almost all of them with a narrower focus than their predecessors, indicating that those associations with a precisely defined member market are in demand and succeeding. Their mission is clearer with a well-defined market. Their value proposition is stronger because their programs and services are more focused. Their organizations are more efficient because their resources are more concentrated. Their communications improve with more targeted messaging. Their competitiveness is enhanced with efforts dedicated to a more distinct market.

Contributing Factors

It's not just the structural changes in the market due to consolidation and specialization that are driving the change in associations. Two other trends identified in Chapter One come into play. Increased competition and higher member expectations team up with member market changes to create an environment that is hostile to the broad-based association trying to serve a complex and diverse member market.

In fact, serving a broadly defined member market is a competitive disadvantage because a broad market almost certainly has a variety of players and constituencies. They have different needs and high expectations. And when it comes to members who support the association for the "greater good," you can count them on one hand and have fingers left over. This means services, advocacy, and activities are required for multiple interests. And that means managing multiple programs, more complex organizational structures, and resources allocated to multiple initiatives. Where will you be more effective: serving a simple market or a complex market?

While the broad-based association spreads its resources in serving multiple constituencies, many of its competitors are focused on solely serving a finite market or sharply focused on providing a single product or service to the broader market. In the worst case scenario for a broad-based association, the competitor is sharply focused on providing a single product to a very tightly defined market. In this case, the traditional association has little, if any, chance of delivering a meaningful rival product or service that can compete with a single-service provider concentrated on a niche market.

For example, the typical construction association is in the government relations business, the education business, the safety business, the insurance business, the convention business, the industry information business, and the project plan business. The project plan business, which has been traditionally delivered through plan rooms where the association housed the blueprints for upcoming projects, has gone digital and is delivered via the internet. iSqFt is an entrepreneurial company that quickly responded to the demand for online construction documents and promotes itself as "the leader in preconstruction." Their singular focus on this emerging opportunity gave them a huge advantage over hundreds of construction associations that had multiple other businesses to manage in addition to project planning.

Member scrutiny of dues and value received is another contributing factor. As members increasingly question their return on investment, it is likely they will question why they are paying dues when they don't need, use, or value a significant percentage of the association's offerings. There is no value in programs or services that a member doesn't use. Today's members question why they are paying to support programs and services designed for members in other segments—particularly if those segments are of marginal importance or represent competition to them.

The Member Market Mindset

The traditional mindset regarding the member market is driven by two factors: habit and a penchant for growth.

Association leadership and management habitually continue to think in traditional terms. They have a predisposition to the member market as it has been. "We serve CPAs." "Automobile dealers are our members." "We serve physicians." "Manufacturers are our members." And so on. They act as if nothing has changed, when the reality is that fundamental and irreversible changes have taken place in their member markets, which will continue to evolve.

Next, most associations are intent on growth. "The bigger, the better" and "The more, the merrier" seem to describe the common bias. This thinking drives efforts to stretch and expand the scope of membership. There are many reasons for the drive for more members: additional revenue, increased clout, more prestige, advantages of scale. And who can argue with growing the membership? It would be un-American to question membership growth. Why would you *not* want to increase the membership?

This begs the question: Won't this approach to a more narrowly defined member market mean we will be smaller and have fewer resources? Perhaps, but if so, the association's resources will be more concentrated, the value of belonging significantly enhanced, retention rates improved, and targeted market share higher. An even more significant question is: Is an association's mission to be bigger or to serve its members? If you look at associations with focused member markets, you will generally find that many are effective in attracting industry or supplier support precisely because those companies are also targeting that segment or niche and they find that their marketing dollars are optimized by being focused on their target market.

One final proponent of membership growth: the affiliate or associate member. These suppliers of products or services to the primary member are likely to be more interested in a larger association membership base than a smaller one. They would prefer access to more potential customers or clients. They want more readers of publications and websites for their advertising, more members to see their directory listings, and more attendees at meetings and exhibitions. And associations want the revenue offered by associate or affiliate dues, advertising, sponsorships, and exhibit income.

In our experience, little, if any, critical assessment is made of how viable it is to continue to serve the market as it has evolved. Given the major changes in the way markets are composed and how the players in the market have changed, can an association really serve all car dealers? All CPAs? All manufacturers? All physicians? Frankly, have associations ever really done a good job of serving these entire markets as they defined them in the past, when it was far more homogeneous and had considerably more in common? A closer look will probably reveal that associations did a good job of serving the majority, but there were always segments or constituencies that were underserved as well as those that had varying needs and interests.

We have encountered few—actually, we remember only one or two—serious discussions about the opportunity cost of attempting to recruit and serve member segments with a marginal affinity to the association's value proposition. What if that time and effort were expended on the member segment where we have the strongest value? What are we *not* doing for our most aligned members while we are fiddling around trying to find value for companies or professionals with a weak link to our primary programs and services? Countless dollars, staff time, and volunteer effort have been allocated to the fringes of membership with little to show for it. These valuable financial and human resources would have been better deployed by strengthening the services and benefits to a more tightly defined member market.

Rarely, if ever, do volunteer leaders or staff challenge or question the current thinking about who the member is and should be. Instead, they say, "It's the member market we've always served."

If any consideration is given to the scope of membership, it is far more likely that the board or management will think of extending the association's boundaries rather than reducing them. And you know what? Most of these efforts fail miserably. In our consulting work, we have encountered many associations that decided that they could increase their membership by recruiting members from adjacent constituencies or related markets. Most of these recruitment campaigns have been unsuccessful. What does that tell you? It tells you that the association is probably already overextended, offering little value to members at their periphery. Now when they try to go beyond borders where their value is already limited, they find that potential members see little or no value in belonging to the association. It is highly likely that with the association market being mature, as a general rule, there is another association already serving that market anyway.

The Member Market of the Future

The member market has changed, and it will never again be as it was. Member expectations have increased and are not likely to relax in the future. Members, like consumers, will not accept an inferior product once exposed to an innovation that performs better. In fact, improvement increases the appetite for additional improvement, not regression. Are we going back to land-based phone lines? Faxes? The U.S. Postal Service? Propeller-driven airplanes? The competition in the marketplace has heated up and is not going away. Because the race for relevance is on, it is time to rethink the member market.

How broad a constituency can your association effectively serve? What is the right size of your member market? Where should you draw the line around your target member market so that you can concentrate resources for maximum performance? What member segments or constituencies are marginal and should be purposefully abandoned?

This is about challenging the way you think, challenging years of conventional wisdom, challenging a mindset. Making important changes in how you define your market in the future is critical for your association's vitality in the coming years. Chances are, the tougher your decisions today, the greater the rewards for your association as a whole tomorrow.

Not a "Core" Member

In advocating that associations more precisely define and limit the member market, we have purposely avoided calling it a "core market."

Some associations have dealt with the challenge of an increasingly diverse member market by differentiating "core" members from "noncore" or "secondary" members. This is an attempt to recognize and respond to the difficulties of serving multiple constituencies and provides guidance about which members are a priority and which are most important.

The concept is commendable, but flawed. First of all, who wants to be a noncore member? Who wants to be a second-class citizen? Who wants to pay dues to an association that says, "We focus on our core members first, and then if we have extra time, we can serve members on the periphery."

More importantly, it is flawed because it is tinkering. It is proposing a compromise solution that doesn't address the essence of the problem. What is required is a radical departure in thinking, not a Band-Aid®. Associations need to rigorously define the member market where they can provide a unique added value and walk away from members who don't fit. If they don't, they will continue to be distracted and will disperse increasingly scarce resources.

We avoid defining a core member market because it implies that there are other members that the association should be serving. Instead, we encourage associations to precisely define the member market: one that shares a high level of common needs and interests, a member market that is narrow and limited by design. Associations that thrive will exercise unwavering discipline in focusing solely on that member market.

No Nirvana

There is no perfect member market. Even with a precisely defined market, associations still will be confronted with member differences, and these differences must be addressed. The National Council of State Housing Agencies has only 54 agency members. You would think that this is the perfect homogenous group. Not so. The agency members differ significantly: large versus small states; single-family versus multifamily housing programs; agencies of the state government versus independent agencies; rural states versus states with metropolitan populations, and so on.

The key to success is focusing energy and resources on meeting well-defined member needs and problems rather than trying to be all things to all people in hopes of maximizing membership and dues income. In many cases, this requires a reexamination of the market and important decisions about whom the association can best serve.

Getting Started

Though difficult, narrowly defining your member market often makes future decision making easier. Here are 11 questions designed to stimulate analysis and introspection to help you look at your member market from a critical perspective, challenge conventional thinking, and get leadership and staff out of their comfort zones. They should be used to create a dialogue around the issue of what the member market should be going forward. It's best to supplement the discussion with statistics, trends, historical data, and other factual information designed to help participants make an objective, rather than a subjective, evaluation.

First are questions about the market:

1. What major industry or professional changes or trends have resulted in changes in the profile (size, scope, operating model, etc.) of the member?

2. How many distinct member segments or constituencies are there in our member market today?

3. What would segmentations of the member market reveal if you compared 1960 and 2010?

4. What assumptions are you making about the member profile or characteristics in the coming years?

Next are questions about the membership:

5. What membership segments have high nonrenewal rates? Why?

6. What potential membership segments are more difficult to recruit? Who are "hard sells" in your recruitment campaigns? Why?

7. What membership segments give the association low satisfaction rates in member surveys? Why?

8. What member segments have membership in another industry association or professional society? Why?

9. What member segments have low participation rates in your association's meetings and conferences? Which have low utilization of fee-for-service offerings? Why?

10. If you have special interest groups, sections, or divisions, which are the most successful and which ones struggle? Which draw membership and participation and which don't? Why?

11. Knowing what you know today, what extensions of the member market undertaken by the association in the past did not produce the anticipated results? If you could turn the clock back and remake the decision, would you? Why?

If you are unable to answer the above questions, you have some homework to do. You are operating in a comfort zone that is based on hunches and assumptions that are more likely to be wrong than right. There is likely to be some harsh reality to face once the true situation is known.

Leading Change

The findings from the responses to the questions above will give the association an initial reality check. And the attitude of the leadership and staff to the process will be revealing. It may show that there is some support for change, but it may also show that resistance to change is high. Regardless of the response, you will know where you stand with important stakeholders and this will help you develop the appropriate approach. For example, if there appears to be some initial agreement that the analysis requires further action, you can proceed with some confidence. If there is strong resistance, you know that you will have to build a very strong case. And if the reaction is mixed, you know who supports change and who is tied to the status quo. This information is essential intelligence as you move forward.

While each association's situation is different, the following steps are proposed as a guide on how to proceed with rationalizing your member market:

Review the responses to the 11 questions. Where did you have good information? Where did you rely on guesses or assumptions? Determine what information gaps are important to fill and use surveys or other techniques to compile the information you need to make sound decisions.

Collect good data to make your case. It is too easy to poke holes in a proposal that lacks facts, and conversely, it is difficult to argue against hard numbers.

Complete a matrix that presents a well-thought-out analysis of the current member market. A sample is provided on the next page, but you should feel free to modify it based on your particular association's unique situation. It is an analytic guide, not a cookie cutter tool.

This matrix was designed to assist associations in a critical evaluation of their member market. The numerical assessment is intended to reduce

Member Segment or Constituency	Number of Members	Percentage of Membership	Membership Trend	Market Share	Satisfaction or Value Ratings (survey findings)	Retention Rate	Use or Participation in Top 3 Programs	Membership in Other Associations	Total Relevance Rating

bias and emotions. The "forced choice" approach eliminates the tendency to give high ratings across the board.

Here's how to use the matrix:

List the member segments in the vertical column. Then, list the analytical components in the horizontal columns. The following are proposed as a guide and much of the information required will have been accumulated in the response to the 11 questions (or in the process of filling the important data gaps):

- Satisfaction or value rating;
- Size (number of members in the segment);
- Percentage of total membership;
- Membership trend;
- Market share;
- Membership in other association(s);
- Level of participation or utilization in top three programs and services;
- Retention rate; and
- Total "Relevance Rating."

Total the number of all member segments or constituencies. Divide the total by 5 for your "rating quota." For example, if you have 10 member segments or constituencies listed, you divide by 5 and your rating quota is 2. The quota limits the number of constituencies you can give high rankings, and forces you to give lower rankings to segments.

Under each vertical column heading, you should assign a number from 1 to 5 to each program or service. A "5" is the highest or most favorable rating and a "1" the lowest. However, you must assign ratings limited by your rating quota. In the example above with 10 member segments or constituencies, you can give only two segments a "5" rating, two segments a "4" rating and so on. (Yes, two segments must be given a "1.") We recommend that you fill in your two "5s" first, then the lowest two "1s." Then go back and fill in your two "4s," your two "2s," and two "3s".

Total the ratings horizontally and rank them from the highest total to the lowest using an Excel worksheet. The total rating is the segment's or constituency's "Relevance Rating." (To download a free, ready-to-use copy of this matrix, go to www.raceforrelevance.com.)

Make your case for the optimum member market and your rationale. The relevance ratings will provide valuable support for your proposal. Your case should include:

- A precisely defined member market for the association going forward and the segment(s) that represent the greatest opportunity for the association to add value and deliver return on their investment;

- Estimates of current potential members in the market as defined and 5- to 10-year forecasts of the number of potential members in the target market;

- Projections of recruitment results and retention rates for the new member market;

- The segments that should be purposefully abandoned; and

- A demonstration of what resources will be freed up by abandoning segments and how those resources will be reallocated and concentrated on the member market of the future.

Gain board consensus on the member market of the future and the actions necessary to capitalize on it. Remember, you have a competency-based five member board.

Institutionalize the decisions. This is probably best accomplished by changing the membership criteria in the association's bylaws. You want to make sure that your decisions stick and that member market "creep" does not return.

Monitor response, measure success, and modify plans as necessary. The matrix is a helpful tool in doing this on an ongoing basis.

We're not suggesting lurching from one market to the next or changing your market year to year in an attempt to find what works. We are suggesting you narrowly define your market, assess its needs, and position yourself to meet these needs. You'll be more successful when you do and it will be easier to identify the programs, services, and activities of most interest to your members, the topic covered in the next chapter.

Radical Change: Rationalizing the Member Market

ASSOCIATION: Texas Trial Lawyers Association

BUDGET: $6 million

NUMBER OF STAFF MEMBERS: 26

NUMBER OF MEMBERS: 2,200

CASE STUDY:

"We were filling the bucket but we had a valve open on the bottom," says Tiffany McGee, senior director of membership and fund development for the Texas Trial Lawyers Association (TTLA). Though the association recruited 450 new members a year, retention was around 80 percent, which meant membership overall was stagnant. The 2002 statewide election changed everything.

"Republicans swept every office in Texas," recalls Tiffany. "And we lost many major tort reform battles. Suddenly our members' livelihoods were threatened." The association raised extraordinary amounts of money for the legislative fight that ensued and to address a constitutional amendment to be voted on by the general public. Though all members benefited from the association's advocacy, Fellowship members (who paid the highest dues), bore the brunt of the financial burden. According to McGee, that's when it became clear that "we had to spread the responsibility among our greater group of members beyond just the Fellowship members."

Prior to the election, the philosophy at TTLA was to keep dues low, provide a lot of services and be all things to trial lawyers. But a conversation among the executive director, the membership director, and past presidents had been quietly taking place. What if TTLA offered more specialized services for greater dues—even if the tradeoff meant fewer members? It was a bold discussion—one that required rationalizing the member market and one that took on a sense of urgency after the election left Texas trial lawyers reeling.

Though general membership retention was around 80 percent, retention among Fellowship members was 98 percent. McGee notes, "It was very easy to see the enlightenment and the loyalty and dedication of the people who gave the greatest amounts of money." The group began to wonder if being all things to all trial lawyers was more of a detriment than a help when it came to building a strong organization. They decided to find out.

TTLA proposed a hefty dues increase along with a change in membership levels and held a facilitated discussion about the proposal. "We made sure that we had all segments of the membership involved in the discussion," says McGee. "We had had a really good cross section, so that's the data we used when we made the change."

Though the association predicted a loss of membership in the 30 to 35 percent range, it also predicted an overall increase in revenue due to membership changes. The gutsy move paid off. "We hit it right on the nose," says McGee. "We lost 35 percent of our members, so we had a 65 percent retention rate the first year. The following year it was about 78 percent. Since then, we've been hovering around 88 percent. At the time of the change, our revenue basically doubled because the majority of our members moved into the top dues category."

Changing association philosophy isn't easy. But to remain relevant it's often necessary. McGee offers the following advice: "Listen to your members and listen to your stakeholders, but also look at the numbers. Be really honest about the needs of your association. And never back down from the value of your organization."

What's the value of your organization to your members? If you can't articulate it, your members won't likely recognize it either. And if you can articulate it, are you leveraging it to the fullest extent?

Radical Change: Providing Consulting Services to Members

ASSOCIATION: National Association for Printing Leadership

BUDGET: $6.5 million

NUMBER OF STAFF MEMBERS: 30

NUMBER OF MEMBERS: 2,800

CASE STUDY:

Mergers, acquisitions, consolidations, and firm closures led to a change in thinking for the National Association for Printing Leadership (NAPL). Seeing a bleak future with fewer players in the market, the association decided to concentrate less on overall market share and to focus more on "share of member." The philosophical change, from a typical association program and service structure to a consulting organization with a membership component, internally moved the organization from one with a questionable future to an entirely new association model. The group now operates as a consultancy, hiring industry specialists to partner with members. As the work with a member increases, so do dues, resulting in higher income for the association. More importantly, members are experiencing stellar returns as a result of the association's consulting services, even in a challenging market.

Printing has changed tremendously over the years, as evidenced by the fact that the association has changed names three times. The organization began in 1933 as the National Association of Photo Lithographers. In 1979, the association became the National Association of Printers and Lithographers. Twenty years later the association's focus changed to developing leaders inside member companies. Thus, the change to its current moniker: the National Association for Printing Leadership.

Market changes, as well as a new generation of business leaders focused more on getting a return on investment for their dues investment, drove both the name and philosophical change. When the philosophical change occurred, the association added consulting in addition to traditional member services. According to president and CEO Joe Truncale, "We didn't make it an all or nothing bet at the outset." But the results quickly proved the new direction was a winner. The group produced $200,000 in consulting revenue the first year, and the number has grown every year since. In 2010, the association projects it will generate $2.4 million in consulting income.

Entry level dues are $1,200 per year. Members using the consulting services pay $3,000 per month for however long they use the advanced services. NAPL works with client members to determine their needs, which range from help with sales, marketing, and finance to mergers and acquisitions. Notes Truncale, "When you think about that…who could you hire for $36,000 a year to provide this kind of guidance and direction?"

Though numbers are important, it's not just the association's income that matters. Even more importantly, says Truncale, are the numbers of the member companies they've worked with. "It wasn't just our numbers. It was the numbers of the companies that we were working on and the improvement that took place inside those businesses that really helped us turn the corner in terms of convincing everyone this is the right thing to do."

Ultimately, the consulting work done by NAPL staffers benefits the entire membership, as staff experiences are developed into knowledge products, worksheets, and other tools available to all members.

Truncale advises association executives to take their time in finding their organization's "biggest and best future" by "concentrating on their core strength and trying to identify the association's unique abilities that can be matched up with an emerging need in the marketplace." Once that's done, he suggests "laying out a careful plan and direction and staying with it." Then, "communicate, communicate, communicate."

Though NAPL's new orientation is crystal clear to him, he finds it's not always so with leaders who have distractions and commitments outside the association. He notes, "When you think you've communicated so much your leaders are sick of hearing you say it, say it again." Doing so helps keep volunteers focused on core strengths and helps prevent the "focus drift" that occurs within many organizations and weakens their value to members.

CHAPTER SIX

Rationalize Programs, Services, and Activities

Does Volume Equal Value?

The typical trade association or professional society tries to do too much. They attempt to provide a complete menu of programs, services, products, meetings, events, publications, and activities. Associations continue to add to their offerings and rarely discontinue any. The result of these practices is in an ever-expanding array of the average association's benefits and fee-for-service programs.

Despite the expanding scope of products and services, the "Pareto Principle" (80 percent of consequences stem from 20 percent of the causes) continues to rule over any association's range of service offerings. Also known as the "80/20" rule, the principle projects 80 percent of member value is derived from 20 percent of the benefits offered. So if an association offered 10 programs or activities, two of them would account for 80 percent of the value received. What is the purpose of continuing to offer the other eight? Given that they generate only 20 percent of the value, why sustain them? Why do associations continue to spend valuable time and energy when the return is so low? Why don't associations concentrate their efforts on the two products that deliver the overwhelming majority of member value?

The intentions are good: we want to do more for the member. We want to increase the value of belonging. We want to give members more for their dues dollar. We want to keep dues low by offsetting revenue from nondues programs.

Several years ago in a strategic planning session, the question of how many services the association should offer was debated. Some on the board felt that the association was obligated as an association to offer a lot of services. "That's what we are supposed to do as a nonprofit association, aren't we?" Others felt that the association was trying to do too much and as a result, most of its benefits were mediocre and had low member utilization. None of its offerings had exceptionally high use by members. Finally, one member of the board asked, "What is better, a lot of average programs or a few high quality programs? Which would our membership rather have us offer?" We're not sure if he was being serious or facetious. But it didn't make any difference. His peers on the board could not agree on an answer.

This debate is not new. It's been going on for a long time. In 1990, Mark Levin, CAE, CSP, wrote an article on this phenomenon titled "What Is This Stuff?" In it he lamented the trend of associations and professional societies' aggressively adding new products and discounts to build the "value" of membership.

A list of actual association offerings he cited included bumper stickers, fax machine discounts, and discounts on amusement park rides. He commented, "I don't understand how spending time and money to create a laundry list of 'stuff' to put in a brochure does one thing to advance the goals of an association or society." He continued, "Our job is to identify and meet the actual, factual, real-life, they-do-this-for-a-living needs of our members. How does an amusement park discount program do that?"

While some of these examples of program proliferation are extreme, they are symptomatic of the thinking. There is one major underlying assumption that is flawed: that the way to add value to membership is to add more programs, services, and benefits. The more "stuff" the better. In a nutshell, the thinking is that volume equals value.

Some executives are figuring this out. Martin Sirk, CEO of the International Congress and Convention Association says, "Over the years,

I have concluded that my association can never be more than a small segment of its members' lives, so we strive to make that slice of time as valuable, enriching, and constructive as possible." (*Associations Now*, April 2010) The association has eliminated marginal programs, rationed communications, and concentrated resources on core experiences.

The Program and Service Mindset

As with conventional thinking about the member market, the traditional mindset regarding the scope of programs, services, and activities is driven by several factors. Two are closely related to those of the member market mindset: habit and a penchant for growth. There is a lot going on here that you need to be aware of. The current is strong and complex.

First, existing programs and services are often continued without much challenge. It seems that once introduced, programs are granted a lifetime contract. It's like being tenured as a university professor. Programs are continued because of tradition, some type of sacred cow status, or simply inertia. They get factored into the budget and, short of a catastrophe, they are repeated year after year. Sunsetting is considered only in the case of severe financial stress. (More on this later.)

As with the membership mindset, the penchant for growth is at play here as well. A flawed association paradigm shared by many staff and volunteers drives adding services: That's what associations are supposed to do. We're supposed to come up with new ways to provide services and value to the member. We're supposed to add new "stuff," as Levin called it.

The current paradigm is that more is better. Boards, committees, and staff all share this thinking.

Boards seem to be disposed to adding programs and services. It must be in their genetic makeup. Most boards never met a new program or service opportunity they didn't like. One of the biggest contributors to program and service expansion is the chief elected officer with an agenda or "pet project." Their contributions to the profession or the industry during their terms have littered the association landscape with thousands of well-intentioned but usually half-baked ideas about a new activity, benefit, or initiative. We even know of associations that have a line item in the annual budget to accommodate a chief elected officer's personal perquisite. Once the program gets started, no one is around to pull the plug or turn it off.

Committees have the same propensity to add new stuff. Show me a committee that doesn't want to recommend a new service or activity. For many, it is their reason for existence. Examine committee chairs who have received an association award and you will usually find a new service or initiative as the reason for their being acknowledged. And many committees are led by politically savvy individuals who know how to work the board and staff to get their proposals adopted. Once approved, the same committee leadership now has an ownership in the new program or service that operates as a major barrier to discontinuing it if it doesn't work or becomes obsolete. They will use that same political savvy to block efforts to discontinue their pet service or program.

And staff joins in. Adding new programs and benefits is seen as an important accomplishment. What staff member would not want to be recognized as the one behind a new service? When it comes to working with a committee or task force, what is a staff member to gain by discouraging a volunteer leader with an idea to add a new benefit? And show us an association executive's résumé that doesn't highlight the programs and services they added during their time on the job. Everybody is in the game.

Programs and services are often increased to "meet the diverse interests of the membership." The association increases its offerings for different interests within the membership. But ask, "What services are targeted to which segment?" and more often than not, the response is vague and lacks supporting data. It is based on assumptions and conjecture that would fail even modest scrutiny.

The Power of a Narrow Product and Service Line

To remain relevant and vital, association leadership and management must think differently about the range of the association's programs and activities. They must increasingly recognize the power of a tightly focused menu of services and initiatives. They need to learn that concentrating resources on the most important member benefits will pay off and that continuing to offer a broad range of benefits disperses resources, inhibits the association from excelling in any one area, and exposes the association to increasing competition that is likely focused on a single product or service. They will see the wisdom in Johann Wolfgang von Goethe's words: "Things that matter most must never be at the mercy of things that matter least."

The role of resource concentration in successful strategy has been restated and reinforced for centuries. In 200 BC, Sun Tzu wrote, "Concentrate your energy and hoard your strength."

Between 1816 and 1830 Carl Philipp Gottlieb von Clausewitz wrote his book *On War,* the seminal work on contemporary military strategy. In it he writes, "There is no higher or simpler law for strategy than keeping one's forces concentrated." And, "We must focus the largest possible number of troops at the decisive point in the engagement." Finally, "It sounds unbelievable, and yet it has happened a hundred times over, that troops have been divided and separated merely according to some vague sense of how things are conventionally done, without a clear understanding of why it is being done."

In his 1973 book *Management: Tasks, Responsibilities and Practices,* Peter F. Drucker wrote, "Wherever we find a business that is outstandingly successful, we will find that it has thought through the concentration alternatives and has made a concentration decision," as well as, "The worst thing to try to do is a little bit of everything. This makes sure that nothing is being accomplished. It is better to pick the wrong priority than none at all."

In his *Competitive Strategy,* Michael Porter wrote in 1980, "The desire to grow has the most perverse effect on strategy.... pressures to grow or apparent saturation of the target market leads managers to broaden the position by extending product lines, adding new features, imitating competitors' popular services...." He also observed, "Through incremental additions of product varieties, incremental efforts to serve new customer groups (read "member"), and emulation of rivals' activities, the company (read "association") loses its competitive position."

In the 1990s Oren Harari wrote, "An organization that offers a wide, diversified menu of mediocre or commodity products and services is not in a value mode. The moment an organization tries to be all things to all people, the focus on innovation and delivery blurs, identity and priorities become confusing and efficiencies plummet."

In his 2001 best-seller *Good to Great*, Jim Collins proposed the "Hedgehog Concept" attributing the performance of great organizations to disciplined focus in their practices and avoidance of distractions and diversification.

Despite the strategic value of focus, associations have not gotten the message.

The Void in Association Program and Service Thinking

There is a major void in most association thinking about programs and services: resources. It can be argued that few association leaders or managers have a full grasp of the resources necessary for any of their association's particular programs or services.

Nothing illustrates the point better than the lack of thinking behind the simple statement, "It won't take that much to support that new benefit." This comment has resulted in the approval of thousands of marginal or worthless association programs or benefits. This statement is a debilitating disease that needs to be eradicated. A board or committee member will throw it out, and no one will challenge it. If staff questions the resources or effort required, they will appear to be defensive or attempting to avoid work. So they sit quietly knowing full well that the volunteer has no idea of what it will take and is underestimating what is actually going to be involved.

Little consideration is given to what is required to develop, maintain, deliver, support, and market association programs and services. An analysis of the resources required for a proposed new service would seem to be a given. But few are conducted and they are usually limited and incomplete. Many proposed programs are approved without even a cursory evaluation. Once instituted, a review of resources necessary to support existing programs and activity is generally only undertaken during the budgeting process. And this review considers only financial resources.

Certainly, financial resources are significant and important. But a true resource assessment must go beyond just the costs to develop, maintain, deliver, support, and market association programs and services. There are four levels of resources for any association program or activity: direct costs, human resource costs, overhead expenses, and intangible costs.

For starters, most associations allocate only direct costs when evaluating the margin or "profit" on a program or service. This approach is so flawed that it defies explanation. In his article "The Value of Knowing the Cost" (*Associations Now,* Feb. 2010), Andrew Lang, CPA, writes, "As a student of association finance, I am mystified by the number of organizations that do not know the true cost of what they are selling. If you ask association executives if they know the cost of a particular product or service, most will say 'yes.' However, on further inquiry, the vast majority are referring to the direct cost, and often enough, only the out-of-pocket direct cost. All too frequently, associations that do not know the full cost of what they are selling are selling at a loss."

It seems obvious that to get a true reading on a program or service's margin or "profitability" that you have to include all the costs associated with what it takes to develop, maintain, deliver, support, and market an association program, service, or activity. And yet many associations conveniently skip over this step.

Human resources are one of the association's most valuable assets. This includes the association's volunteers, paid staff, and independent contractors or consultants. The board and CEO know what their staff's general responsibilities are. But they usually don't know how their time and effort are allocated to programs and activities. When a board does look into how staff time is apportioned to various programs and services, the reaction is usually surprise at the amount of time required. Boards generally underestimate time commitments and effort. Some of this is due to staff's being reluctant to spell it out, concerned that they may be seen as looking for sympathy, appearing inefficient, or exaggerating the time it takes. But mostly it is the board that tends to dismiss the time and effort necessary. An association's staff and increasingly scarce volunteer resources are far too valuable not to have a handle on. You can't optimize these resources if you don't know how they are being deployed.

Overhead is a part of the cost to develop, maintain, deliver, support, and market association programs and services. Staff needs office space, equipment, utilities, and supplies. Inventory needs to be stocked somewhere. While sometimes difficult to calculate, overhead can't be ignored.

The intangible resources are the most difficult to identify and even more challenging to quantify. Staff payroll and benefits are one thing, but what about their energy, enthusiasm, or creativeness? We can account for volunteer time, but what about the intellectual property they bring to the association? What about the credibility board members or committee chairs bring to the organization? How about the value of the synergy that results from volunteer and staff collaboration? It could be easily argued that these are much more valuable resources than direct costs and overhead. So why do associations not pay more attention to how they are put to work?

A strategic approach to association program and service thinking requires skillful, creative, and disciplined use of the association's resources. That cannot be done when prevailing thinking fails to take the time to understand and account for all of the resources that go into a program or service. This is an important first step that will then illuminate the potential of realigning resources so that they are concentrated on the programs and services that have the highest value and on activities that will strengthen the association's ability to deliver that value.

Opportunity Cost

Most associations would like to increase the staff and funding for their major programs or services. Generally, there are never enough resources to devote to high priority, highly valued programs, services, or association systems.

Government advocacy efforts could be strengthened with a stronger grassroots effort if additional staff were allocated to identifying, recruiting, and mobilizing members. Information systems and databases could be better leveraged if additional funding were available. Educational programming and delivery systems could be upgraded if staff could be expanded. Meeting and conference attendance could be boosted if marketing budgets could be increased. The foundation's fundraising performance could be doubled if there were additional development personnel.

In almost all cases, the resources are available. No additional dues or income is required. The staffing and funding exist; they are just being allocated to other programs, services, or activities. This is the opportunity cost of trying to do too much. This is the opportunity cost of being spread too thin. This is the opportunity cost of lacking the discipline to concentrate resources on key result areas.

Once an analysis of the association's resource allocations is made, strategic questions can then be posed. Consider the following to create a dialogue on the subject:

- Are we allocating resources to focus on opportunities to add value?

- Do we allocate resources primarily based on history and tradition or based on tomorrow's opportunities?

- Are we concentrating resources on key result areas that respond to the needs of our members?

- Are we allocating resources to what we know how to do versus what we should be doing?

- Are we allocating sufficient resources to the development and testing of new programs, services, and delivery mechanisms?

- Where are resources being allocated with marginal return?

- Where has the performance of a program been far short of our original expectations?

- Which services and activities are not optimizing the resources required to support them?

- How can we reduce or discontinue allocating resources to the under-performers so that we can reallocate them to programs and activities that will produce returns going forward?

How Many Businesses Can an Association Be in?

Today's typical association attempts to be in multiple "businesses." In most cases, this results in a little bit of this, a little bit of that, and a lot of nothing.

It is not uncommon for a trade association or professional society to be in five, seven, 10, or more distinct businesses. They are in the education and professional development business. The information business. The government advocacy business. The publishing business. The public relations business. The networking business. The community service or social responsibility business. The standards or certification business. The group discount business. The convention and exhibition business. The research business.

In many respects, they are like department stores. Department stores were once dominant players in retailing. But then along came specialty stores like The Gap, Foot Locker, Bed Bath & Beyond, Toys "R" Us, and Williams-Sonoma. And accompanying them were the off-price malls, where discounted surplus inventory was sold. And then along came the big discounters like Walmart, Target, and Costco. And then came the online retailers like Amazon, Dell, and Office Depot. Department stores lost major market share to all these competitors. They could not compete with their extensive assortment offerings. They could not compete with their pricing models. They tried to stay in a lot of businesses. It just doesn't work. And they are losing the race.

Associations are in the same position as department stores, trying to stay in many businesses. In doing so, they are vulnerable to specialized competitors for everything from educational programs to trade shows, vulnerable to alternative sources of industry and market information (most of it available free on the internet), vulnerable to networking options available through social media. The department store model is failing today and so is the traditional association model.

The vast majority of trade associations and professional societies are relatively small, particularly when compared to for-profit companies. According to ASAE's *Operating Ratio Report, 13th Edition* (2008), the median reported gross revenue is $3.8 million. Of the 660 associations reporting, 52.8 percent have gross revenue of $5 million or more and 15.5 percent have gross revenue of $1 million or less.

Of 1,111 associations reporting in the *2006 ASAE Policies and Procedures in Association Management: A Benchmarking Guide,* the breakdown of staff is as follows:

Number of Full-Time Equivalent Staff	Number of Associations Reporting
1–2	150
3–5	214
6–10	194
11–29	272
30–99	204
100+	78

By far the majority of associations have 29 or fewer staff members. How many businesses can these staffs handle? How many businesses can they run well? How many businesses can they manage that will meet the increasing expectations of their members and effectively compete with other providers?

How many businesses can a $1 million, $2 million, or even $5 million trade association or professional society be in? How many businesses can they support in a meaningful way?

Some will argue that there are successful broad-based companies. Why can't associations emulate their approaches? For starters, most broad-based companies are very large. They have revenues that make an average association's annual income look like a pittance and far more employees than the average association has members. For example, Proctor and Gamble has $78.9 billion in annual revenues and 127,000 employees. Amazon has $24.5 billion and 31,200 employees. Kellogg's has $12.6 billion and 31,000 employees. Associations are simply not in the same league.

Recent reports indicate that even the behemoth consumer product companies are learning that more is not always better. According to the *Wall Street Journal* (Aug. 23, 2010), after years of expanding product lines, consumer-goods companies are pruning their portfolios. They have found that proliferating products "often leads to bloated product portfolios that raise a company's costs, reduce supply-chain efficiency, confuse consumers, and lead to shortages of popular products."

For those of you who want to be the Walmart of your profession or industry, start your exploration of this strategy with a comprehensive list of all the businesses and services that you will have to offer to be a "full-service" association. Then ask yourself some questions. Do you have, or can you acquire, the expertise required to competitively offer each service? Do you have the capital required to buy or develop these businesses? Do you have the marketing skills to effectively promote a broad range of diverse programs? Are you willing to compete head-to-head with your biggest supplier or associate members? For most associations, the answer to these questions is likely to be "no." (And just for the record, Walmart has $408.1 billion in annual revenues and 2.1 million employees.)

Another concern we encounter in advocating for a narrow service and program line is the fear of having "all your eggs in one basket." We're willing to bet that a close look will find that a few, perhaps only one or two, products or services are generating net revenue. While the association may have the appearance of many eggs in multiple baskets, many are subsidized either by dues or net revenue from one or two winners, so the reality is that the organization has all its eggs in one or two baskets. Where is the comfort in this situation? We say focus your efforts on getting your eggs in the right basket.

Communication Consequences

Rarely have we encountered an association or society that did not lament the low member awareness of its programs, services, and activities. They complain that members don't know about all the good services the association offers. They grumble that members don't know all the important things that the association is doing on their behalf. They shake their heads in frustration when member survey results indicate high rates of "not aware" responses on heavily promoted services. Members say they need education; the association promotes educational seminars in every newsletter, but the same small core show up. Members complain about the high cost of insurance and the association offers a group insurance program that is the best in the market and has been marketed consistently since it was introduced five years ago. Yet only 20 percent of the members use it. Why don't they know about these and participate?

Why? Because the association is trying to do too much. The association has to communicate and promote a long list of services and benefits. And when you try to communicate and promote a long and varied menu of programs and services, you create clutter and your effectiveness is diminished significantly.

This consequence of trying to do too much was identified by the late Peter F. Drucker in his 1973 book *Management: Tasks, Responsibilities, and Practices.* He referred to it as one of the "downsides of diversification" and wrote, "Complexity creates communication problems."

What is more effective: communicating one product or two products? What is more effective: communicating a narrow range of products in a single category that complement each other or a wide range of products that have little in common?

The typical association attempts to communicate a wide range of disparate programs and services: education and professional development seminars, information, government advocacy, magazines, newsletters, public relations programs, peer networking, community service or social responsibility activities, standards, certifications, group discounts, conventions, exhibits, research, and more.

When presented with the long list of association offerings, members' eyes glaze over. You lose them after the first three or four items. If you don't think so, try this. Sit down with a few members and give them a list of all of your association's services and ask them to look it over for five minutes. Then take the list away and ask them to enumerate as many as they can. Will they be able to recall half of them?

While the list of association programs and services grows for all the reasons enumerated above, little, if any, thought is given to the communications consequences. No one asks, "Given the difficulty we are experiencing achieving member awareness of our existing programs, what affect will adding another one have? How will we effectively promote it?"

A volunteer leader is likely to say, "It won't take that much. Just mention it in the newsletter." And another contribution to the clutter is made. No one counters that adding another benefit adds to the communication challenge. That the space to promote the new, likely marginal service, would be better devoted to promoting a proven or growing service.

And it gets worse. A common reaction to the frustration with communication and awareness is for the association to increase the frequency of its promotions. They promote more aggressively by increasing the number of emails and mailings. This just exacerbates the problem. Members are bombarded with cluttered communications to the point that they simply turn off the "noise" by adding your association's email sender address to the "Blocked Senders" list or automatically tossing your printed promotions into the round file.

A significant percentage of an association's communications problems are eradicated with the elimination of marginal programs and services. When associations prune out the obsolete, marginal, or declining services and activities, the message becomes simpler. The simpler the message the stronger the ability to communicate.

Want the perfect comparison? Compare any association's home page with Google's home page. You'll see the power of simplicity.

Almost Risk Free

How would you like to be able to make a major, controversial, emotionally-charged change with little or no risk? How would you like a guarantee that if your bold initiative failed, it could somehow be restored or your previous position miraculously recovered?

If you make a mistake and eliminate a program or activity that you should not have, you can simply reintroduce it.

Let's say that even after a thorough analysis and sound decision making, you eliminate one of your association's products and a massive groundswell of member complaint results. Not just a faction, but a widespread protest occurs, with many members protesting and threatening to drop their membership.

No problem. Reinstate the product immediately. "We made a mistake. Our evaluation was flawed. The members have spoken and the product is back as a member benefit." As a matter of fact, you may be able to enhance or improve the product or service in the re-introduction process.

Back in 1985, the Coca-Cola Company introduced "New Coke." An uproar among loyal Coke drinkers ensued. In less than three months,

Coca-Cola management reversed their direction and reinstated "Coca-Cola Classic." The publicity around this blunder significantly raised the brand's profile and demonstrated the bond with the product that management had underestimated. Within six months, Coke's sales were increasing at twice the rate of Pepsi. When a Coca-Cola executive was asked if the new introduction had been a purposely designed ploy to generate the backlash and resulting publicity, he replied, "We weren't smart enough to orchestrate it. But we weren't so stupid as not to capitalize on it once it happened."

If one of the world's largest consumer product companies can recover from a botched product discontinuation, your association or professional society can as well. Though we don't recommend discontinuing a program with the idea of reintroducing it, knowing the option is available often makes it possible to get the go-ahead from volunteer leaders.

In most cases, reposting the benefit on the website is all that will be required. In some instances, it may take time to negotiate a discount program or other third-party benefit. But almost all discontinued programs are easily reversible. And those that take time can be promoted in the interim: "Back in September by popular demand."

This is an aspect of rationalizing your association's programs and services that you should be aware of. It can embolden your resolve and possibly allay the concerns of your opposition. "Hey, if we pull the plug on this service and the members complain, we'll admit our mistake and reinstate it right away."

Getting Started

These seven questions are designed to stimulate dialogue, help you look at your service and product line from a critical perspective, challenge conventional thinking, and get leadership and staff to think differently. They should be used to analyze and project the association's appropriate span of benefits in the future.

- What programs or services have consistently attracted participation by only a small percentage of the members? Which have been used consistently by a high percentage of members?

- Which services or activities failed to measure up to expectations, particularly after several attempts to promote them more effectively? Which services have "taken off" and are more successful than expected?

- Which programs operate at a loss and require subsidies from dues or margins from profitable activities to maintain? If they are valuable, why do we need to subsidize them? Which programs generate strong margins after all resource requirements are allocated?

- What services have peaked in their lifecycle and are mature or in decline? What services are in a growth mode and have the most future potential?

- What services are readily available elsewhere? Where are we the sole provider or market leader? Where do we have low market share? High market share?

- What activities or products are a drain on our resources, particularly those that divert energy and creativity from opportunities? And which services are uniquely matched with the association's intangible resources, like intellectual capital?

- Which service areas are aligned with the market conditions of the past? Which are well matched with current, high-impact market, industry, or professional trends?

Data Gathering

The culture in most associations is averse to change. The tendency is to defend the status quo. Association tradition and politics are simply not geared to disciplined use of resources and making difficult choices. Volunteer leaders don't want to cross peers, and association staff doesn't want to cross volunteer leadership. Most ascribe to "getting along means going along," so "let's not concern ourselves with eliminating his program or her activity. Let's just offer them all." That way, everybody's happy. And then comes the poisonous statement: "It doesn't take that much anyway."

Don't ever forget that tradition and culture in an association require monumental effort and considerable time to change. And the change we propose is a radical departure from conventional thinking. And if change is effected, ongoing effort to inculcate these changes into future leadership and staff will be required. If not, the prospects of backtracking are very high.

Many people will stand in the way. Too many volunteer leaders and staff have a stake in the current programs and services. Many of them participated in their development and are naturally disposed to defending them. Influential members have either supported particular activities or have been long-time users or participants. Most on the board or staff will cling to the mindset that "more services equal more value."

Absent a financial crisis, the pushback to radical change in the service and program line will be substantial. And emotional. And political.

You must not take the first step toward tomorrow's lean range of products and services without supporting data. Data is critical ammunition in your effort. Without data, you are extremely vulnerable to emotional arguments and political maneuvering. Absent factual information, the discussion can be manipulated. Valid information will be the basis for a strong case and is the only effective response to emotional or political appeals.

Once a large meeting of a professional society's board and committees was presented with a plan to eliminate the local chapters. Everybody in the room started out as a chapter leader, so the ties to chapters were especially strong even though many leaders understood that the chapters' time may have come and gone. At one point in the discussion, a past president stood, raised his hand in the air and proclaimed, "The chapters are the very lifeblood of the society! How could we even consider their elimination?"

But then the facts arrived. The president-elect responded, "While I certainly understand your personal and historical attachment to the chapters, I must challenge your premise. Recent attendance figures indicate that in the last year, only 14 percent of the society's members even attended a chapter meeting. That is down from 16 percent last year and a decrease from 24 percent five years ago. How can the chapters be our 'lifeblood' if over 80 percent of members don't go to their meetings?

"In addition, chapter reports indicate that eight of the 11 chapters have openings on their boards that they are unable to fill. Some have had open positions for years. Furthermore, three-fourths of the chapters are unable to recruit members to serve as president. In four or five chapters, board members, officers, and presidents are all being recycled because of the lack of anyone willing to serve. How can the chapters be the society's 'lifeblood' given this situation?

"Finally, the society subsidizes chapter operations with approximately $350,000 a year, which is almost 25 percent of our budget. How can we justify this allocation of resources with declining interest and attendance in chapters when we have opportunities to invest in educational and information technologies that lack funding?"

To venture into a serious discussion of rationalizing the association's services without supporting data is a virtual guarantee of failure. You will need to be prepared to present trend information and utilization rates for underperforming programs. You will need to present an analysis of resource allocations for specific programs and services as well as margin or profit performance—or the lack thereof.

Program and Service Evaluation Matrix

The matrix on the next page was designed to assist associations in a critical evaluation of their programs, services, and activities. Similar to the Member Relevance Matrix, the numerical assessment is intended to reduce bias and emotions. The "forced choice" approach eliminates the tendency to give high ratings across the board.

List all association programs, products, services, and activities in the first vertical column. (Sometimes just putting this list together will be illuminating.) Larger, more complex associations may have to do this by department.

Total the number of all programs, services, products, and activities. Divide the total by 5 for your "rating quota." For example, if you have 30 programs and services listed, you divide by 5 and your rating quota is 6. The quota limits the number of programs you can give high rankings, and forces you to give lower rankings.

Under each vertical column heading, you should assign a number from 1 to 5 to each program or service. A "5" is the highest or most favorable rating and a "1" is the lowest. However, you must assign ratings limited by your rating quota. In the example above with 30 programs and services,

Program, service, product or activity	Relatedness to mission	Life-cycle position	Percentage of members use	Financial results or potential	Effective use of staff and volunteer time	Available from other sources?	Would we start today?	Total

you can give only six programs a "5" rating, six programs a "4" rating and so on. (Yes, six programs must be given a "1.") We recommend that you fill in your six "5s" first, then the six "1s." Then go back and fill in your six "4s," then the six "2s," then six "3s."

Total the ratings horizontally and rank them from the highest total to the lowest using an Excel spreadsheet. Ask why you are continuing the programs and services in the lower third of the evaluation.

Using the matrix will enable you to make an objective comparison of products and services without worrying about the sacred cows and political landmines that often keep associations from evaluating their offerings and eliminating those that have outlived their usefulness or never lived up to their potential. Doing so frees up valuable resources—both financially and from a human resources standpoint. And with greater resources, it's easier to address the technology challenge we discuss in the next chapter.

Radical Change: Managing the Association through a Business Focus

ASSOCIATION: Associated General Contractors of America (AGCA)

BUDGET: $17 million

NUMBER OF STAFF MEMBERS: 65

NUMBER OF MEMBERS: 33,000

CASE STUDY:

Like many associations, in response to member needs and committee ideas, Associated General Contractors of America (AGCA) added to its product and service offerings each year, rarely discontinuing anything in the lineup. But that changed in 2005 when AGCA planned a two-day retreat with its senior managers for the purpose of narrowing the organization's range of products and services.

According to Dave Lukens, chief operating officer, "At the retreat we asked, 'If you were starting from ground zero, what would you invest your time and energy in and what would you do less of?' We came up with five key areas where we thought more energy and more resources would make us more successful."

As a result of the analysis, the association focuses on the five key areas identified at the retreat: safety products, contract documents, management education, supervisory training, and the organization's annual convention. And, Lukens notes, "By emphasizing these and deemphasizing everything else, we significantly increased net nondues revenue."

The change to a more disciplined focus resulted in an internal change as well. Staff is now less reactive and more proactive. "Essentially," says Lukens, "we've said, 'This is your business, and if you need resources, tell us what they are. If you need to develop products, if you need to develop something, let's budget for it.'"

The businesslike focus has also changed the way products are marketed. The association added marketing dollars to promote its products to more than just members. "We're in the business of selling contract documents," says Lukens. So we asked, "If you're going to do that, how do you do it?" And that led to reaching out to members of the American Bar Association who may not be members of Associated General Contractors of America but who do contracts for AGCA members. "We sell a number of our products to almost as many nonmembers as members," Lukens adds.

Product quality has also improved as a result of improved focus. "I'll use our supervisory training program as an example," says Lukens. "The initial workbooks that were developed were actually written by our members. Over time we've migrated away from that. By virtue of taking those over and making it a very high priority, we hired external professional writers and curriculum developers, and so in the end, the 12-unit series of books is much more professionally done and the educational experience is much more professional."

ACGA's new professionalism and willingness to spend money to make money has paid off. But the results weren't instantaneous. "Not all of this really manifested itself in instant revenue," says Lukens. "We had to be patient in some cases, and it took a couple of years before the risks really paid off."

Though the risks produced additional revenue, they also altered staff composition. According to Luken, "The person that was successful here was very focused on pleasing the members, and this activity really isn't about pleasing members. It's about creating membership value, which is, in my mind, a different activity." Some staff were let go but others self-selected. "People decided that this isn't the place that they used to work at, and that's fine." Lukens rewards staff for their efforts and notes that though he doesn't use a formalized bonus structure, "some people have gotten some fairly nice performance bonuses."

Lukens has the support of his leaders in that they recognize there are benefits to hiring and paying professionals, not the least of which has been the increased revenue and professionalism of products, all of which ultimately benefit members. By changing from the inside out, AGCA has added both value and revenue, a combination that's attractive to any association and one that can be replicated by identifying key areas and adopting a disciplined focus.

Radical Change: Narrowing Product Focus

ASSOCIATION: Master Builders of Iowa (MBI)

BUDGET: $4 million

NUMBER OF STAFF MEMBERS: 22

NUMBER OF MEMBERS: 2,100

CASE STUDY:

In 2003, Master Builders of Iowa (MBI) made a bold decision: The association would focus on what it identified as its core capabilities in combination with what members prioritized and let some products and services lapse. By narrowing its focus, the association has been able to develop deeper, more meaningful services for members, including project information and labor relations services. Retention is up by 5 percent as a result.

"We had a list of things that we did that I'm sure no one ever read," says Scott Norvell, executive director. "I know I could get through it only once myself." Though they didn't discontinue programs, staff stopped putting time and effort into those that were of marginal interest or profitability. To determine where its focus should be, MBI surveyed members. When the survey revealed that safety was a priority, the association surveyed again to find out which aspects of safety were the most important to members. The information helped create member services with depth, many of which are delivered via Internet training.

In addition to more fully developing the services that mattered to members, MBI added some services it had previously provided on a fee-basis to the member package. Reworking the basic member package allowed the association to more fully demonstrate the association's value. The result, reports Norvell, is that "our retention and growth in our membership categories has been remarkable considering the economy and considering that the industry is shrinking."

By going deeper with some member services and deemphasizing others, MBI has made it easier to communicate effectively with members. The process has enabled MBI to "be sharper in our communications and probably the most important thing is to understand and communicate our mission and our results since we're not trying to cover everything," says

Norvell. "We're able to track, measure, inform, and communicate what we do with a lot more specificity."

The switch to a narrower focus required a shift in staffing, including expanding the staff in some ways as well as investing in training for current staff. "We had to make sure that we had the appropriate staff and that they were appropriately trained and appropriately motivated to not only answer members' questions but help them figure out questions that they hadn't asked. We had to help them be high performers." The benefit of building a team of high performers is that Norvell depends on staff to innovate and troubleshoot. Though a large portion of board business is done via consent calendar, the bigger discussions focus on providing input when requested via brainstorming and addressing unforeseen complexities as reported by staff.

"Our mission is to be the essential resource for improving member performance and creating a business environment favorable to the construction industry," says Norvell. Adding depth to existing services and creating new ones to meet member needs has made this possible—as has the decision to do less, but to do it better. By deemphasizing less important services, the association has made it possible to excel in areas that matter to members. "We've drilled down to be the very best we can be," Norvell says. And in doing so, the association is making it possible for its members to do the same.

CHAPTER SEVEN

Bridge the Technology Gap and Build a Framework for the Future

The Radical Technology Change

We propose a major redefinition of an association's approach to technology. The adoption and exploitation of technology, particularly information and communication technologies, must become an integral component of the organization's functioning and performance. While technology will always be about the use of tools, crafts, or systems, the scale and potential of the collective power of existing and future technologies requires thought, effort, and resource allocations far beyond those being applied by associations today.

Technology will be to associations what the assembly line has become to manufacturing. In the 1870s, "continuous processing" was an innovation in the meat packing industry. Henry Ford popularized the assembly line in 1914 with his use of it in the production of the Model T. Today, the assembly line is an integral and essential aspect of manufacturing.

Similarly, technology will fundamentally change the way associations deliver value. It will enhance or replace existing delivery systems. It will create new ways to add value that were not conceivable in the past. The effective association of the future will be substantially technology-based.

The current association model is based on members coming to the association: coming to conferences and seminars, coming to committee or task force meetings, coming to fundraising events, and coming to trade shows. The technology-based associations will turn this around and take the association to the member. And with the explosive growth of mobile technology, they will take it to the members wherever they happen to be. It is difficult to ignore that today every association function can be done via technology: meetings, education, networking, fundraising, registrations, everything.

But associations are not going to realize this future if they don't drastically change the way they think about technology. They must significantly increase the resources allocated. They must considerably increase their efforts to adopt technology. In short, they must embrace technology like manufacturers embraced the assembly line.

This chapter is not about which technologies an association should adopt. It is about how associations have to change their thinking about technology and about understanding how it will be critical in positioning their associations for the future. Associations have been slow to adopt technology despite an environment of explosive technological advances—a "technological tidal wave" that swamped associations. (The same tidal wave swamped industries and corporations as well, but that's not our issue.) The consequences are enormous. This is a high stakes race, and a race for relevance that requires a sense of urgency. If associations do not quickly bridge their technology gaps, they risk their relevance to members with each passing day. They will be like a manufacturer that did not adopt the assembly line.

The technology imperative is not going away. It is going to increase in importance. And while associations can't go back and undo the damage that has been done by being slow to adapt, they can move decisively to regain lost ground. The clock is ticking.

Bridging the technology gap is only the first step. It's a critical step, but just the start. Tomorrow's effective association must have a framework that prepares and equips it to maintain its technological relevance. That framework will require a new technological philosophy to support it.

"Technology" Defined

When we refer to "technology" in this chapter, we are generally addressing the full scope of an association's information, communications, and delivery systems as well as the infrastructure required to operate them. It includes all hardware, software, and supporting applications. It includes computers, servers, scanners, and printers. It includes all systems, programming, and application software. And, of course, it includes the technology of the millennium: the internet. It includes all the technologies that support or enable the association's operations, but most important, those that deliver or enhance the delivery of member value: information, communication, education, networking, and other membership deliverables.

Current Situation: Case for Action

In July 2008, Apple opened its App Store. Associations didn't grasp the implications for many, many months. By April 2010, at least 185,000 apps had been created. Application downloads hit *1 billion* in just nine months. How many were developed by associations? One of the first mentions in an association publication was April 2010—nearly two years after apps began appearing. The American Bus Association developed an app for its trade show that offered a daily schedule of events, detailed descriptions of sessions, and links to presenter materials. Attendees could also select the booths they wanted to visit, which were then organized by number for easy navigation.

Though many associations are now jumping on the bandwagon, the lag is typical of what we see in the association world when it comes to technology. Even ASAE admits associations missed the boat on social networks: "Now that we've all stumbled out of the blocks on social media, it's time to get it right." (*Associations Now,* June 2009)

Association Mindset About Technology

Associations have been woefully and consistently slow in adopting technology, from database utilization to digital communications to social media participation. While the focus at the time of writing is on the incredible growth and scale of social media, the technology challenges confronting associations go far beyond this current phenomenon. It is just one more instance of missing the boat in a long line of technology failures in the association community as a whole.

Several reasons are behind the failure of associations to capitalize on technology. In many cases, it has been a combination of multiple factors resulting in a failure to act. But an understanding of what got associations where they are in technology will provide some insight as to how thinking has to change if they are going to catch up and get in the race. There appear to be at least seven aspects of association mentality that resulted in this misadventure with technology.

The Mindset of Boards of Directors

Simply put, the average director was out of touch with many technological developments, particularly those that were internet-based. Most directors were unaware of what was happening. But in some cases, even those who were knowledgeable dismissed emerging technologies as fads or kids' stuff. In our work with boards in the 2000s, we found a high level of unfamiliarity with You Tube, Facebook, LinkedIn, and Twitter well after they had achieved notoriety and significant scale.

David Nour said it well when asked about associations and social networks. "They know of it. But their knowledge, and more importantly their strategic view of it, is really limited." He goes on: "A bunch of people on the board who've got cobwebs hanging off their suits are probably not the best people to determine if social network inspection makes sense. Their members are already there...." (*Associations Now,* May 2009)

Though boards are composed of people with diverse perspectives on technology, some are early adopters, others late adopters. The late adopters were a major roadblock. They even bragged about not having email addresses.

Even having early adopters on the board is not a guarantee of remaining on top of technological advances. In our experience among the early adopters were, unfortunately, individuals who had an exaggerated opinion of their technological savvy. Less knowledgeable directors, somewhat intimidated, deferred technology decisions to those who professed to know what the association's technology direction should be. We worked with one association that spent tens of thousands of dollars and years of effort pursing a volunteer's technological idea that eventually proved to be drastically flawed.

The way associations fumbled the technology opportunity is sufficient by itself to warrant the small, competency-based board proposed in Chapter Two. In our example, one of the key competencies may be a board member that can bring a level of knowledge and understanding of technology's potential and how it might be exploited by the association. Our small, competency-based board is less prone to the downsides of today's technologically disconnected board that got us to the fix we are in.

For planning purposes, it's helpful to know what percentage of members might fall into the early- or late-adopter categories. Based on the examination of a large number of studies in innovation diffusion, in 1995 Everett Rogers proposed a method of adopter categorization in his book *Diffusion of Innovations*. Rogers suggested that the normal curve be divided as follows:

- The first 2.5 percent of the adopters are the "innovators."
- The next 13.5 percent of the adopters are the "early adopters."
- The next 34 percent of the adopters are the "early majority."
- The next 34 percent of the adopters are the "late majority."
- The last 16 percent of the adopters are the "laggards."

It appears that "innovators" and "early adopters" were missing from association and professional society boards. And without innovators on the board, it's difficult to have the confidence and knowledge necessary for making an ongoing commitment to continuing technology upgrades.

Impact Underestimated

Even when the potential was recognized, the impact of technological developments was underestimated. The state of member databases, for example, is an indictment of association management. Customer databases in the for-profit sector have been a powerful marketing tool for decades. But a search for an association that has adequately developed, maintained, and exploited database technology will bring up scant results. Most would agree that the collective membership of an association is the most significant strength of an association or professional society. But associations have failed to capitalize on the technology that would help maintain, grow, serve, and leverage this asset. After working with more than 1,000 trade associations and professional societies, we would be hard pressed to come up with more than a handful that have mastered and exploited database technologies.

Inadequate Resource Allocation

The resources allocated to association technology have been tragically inadequate in most cases. Associations have tended to think of their technology investments as periodic system upgrades made begrudgingly rather than as critical investments in their future. They don't allocate staff with continuity and they hire independent contractors for periodic fixes. Many, if not most, have balked at making system and staff allocations. In some cases, it is simply a matter of not wanting to spend the money. (And at the same time, they have been making annual contributions to their reserves, mortgaging their technological future for the comfort of a larger "rainy day" fund. In our experience, most associations build a surplus for which they have no idea regarding when, or how, they might use it. Ask an association's leadership for their policy about what instances would justify the use of reserves. We'll bet you won't find many that have one.)

Anchored to Traditional Delivery Mechanisms

Technologies that could enable associations to deliver their programs and services more efficiently and quickly encountered pushback from those volunteers and staff who were comfortable with the status quo. A good example would be the change from print to digital delivery. "Members want the newsletter in print form so that they can read it when they want or can take it when they travel." "Members want a printed directory that they can have on their office shelf." But it also affected attitudes toward educational delivery and networking. "Members want a classroom educational environment; they don't want to learn from a computer screen." "Members will always want to meet face-to-face."

Though these statements may be true in some respects, they fail to recognize that many members want 24/7 access to information and education that they can use at their convenience. We were in one meeting when an older member asked a younger member how many print publications the younger one reads. There was an awkward silence as the younger member tried to identify even one. "I don't read print publications," he answered as he held up his iPhone. "I get all my information online."

Lost in the discussion were the enhancements that the technologies offered: the ability to access rich sources of information, the increased speed of delivery and timeliness of information, the ability to track member behavior and preferences.

Leave No Member Behind

One of the most common objections to adopting a new technology involved the segments of membership who were not ready for the change. The best examples were in the change from print to digital delivery. When associations considered converting their printed newsletters to electronic delivery, volunteer leadership and staff both expressed concern that all the members were not ready, that it was too early. In the 1990s we heard over and over again, "We can't switch to an electronic newsletter. We still have members who don't even have email addresses!"

Associations paid a price for this lowest-common-denominator thinking. So they delayed making the change. But the damage was considerable. First, the progressive members were dismayed that the association wasn't adopting the technology. "Why don't they send the newsletter electronically? It would be quicker and cheaper. Why are they still printing it?" And secondly, the longer associations took to capitalize on technological opportunity, the farther behind they got on the next step. Competitors filled the void. Had they been quicker adopters, they would have realized the benefits sooner and been more open to other emerging technologies and their potential. For example, while associations balked at the transition from print to digital, they got behind in the explosive growth in mobile technology.

Fear of Making the Wrong Move

Associations were no different from any other organization in making timely decisions in technology. But it still had an impact. How do you know when to make the investment? How do you know that a better version won't become available shortly? Should you wait a little longer to see what develops? Associations have never been known for speed. So the answers to these questions were generally cautious and conservative in associations, further contributing to delays in decision making.

Reluctance to Give Up Control

First with listservers, and then social networking sites, associations balked at the open nature of online contributions and dialogue. In these formats, the association had little or no control over the conversation. Fears of members libeling or attacking other members under the auspices of the association's forum were not appealing to leaders and executives who were more comfortable with traditional mechanisms where they were in complete control. Legal counsel issued fierce warnings and urged caution. But while associations procrastinated because of these concerns, members went to other online forums and social networks. As a result, many associations ended up on the sidelines.

The Association Philosophy Going Forward

The association technology mindset for the future should reflect the following philosophies:

Capitalizing on the potential of technology, particularly internet-based technology, is an imperative. Association executives and leadership should acknowledge that not becoming more technology-based has significant negative consequences. Technology will shape the way the association is perceived and will be central to its competitive position and critical in winning its race to relevance.

A comprehensive technology plan is essential to guide challenging decision making. Without a plan, an association will continue to flounder. A plan ensures adequate human and financial resources and prioritizes additions, upgrades, and enhancements.

Exploiting technology opportunities will require additional resources. Throwing money at technology is not the answer. But there will be a need for associations to spend a higher percentage of their budgets on technology and divert resources from other areas to meet the need.

Thinking that you can always "catch up later" is an extremely dangerous assumption. While associations procrastinate and delay, other alternative providers and competitors will fill the gap. By the time the association arrives, often the need has been met and the member has an alternative resource.

Taking risks will be required. Associations must commit to becoming better risk takers and accepting inevitable failures and missteps as a necessary cost of the technology imperative.

Do not let members who are late adopters of technology handcuff efforts. Doing so puts the association at risk with the progressive, earlier adopters in the membership who reflect the characteristics of the future member.

Taking Action

There are three areas where associations can take action on the technology front: a "catch up" effort where necessary; institutionalizing a philosophy; and building a framework for the future. The challenges can be met through sound planning, increased resource allocations, and improved risk taking.

Comprehensive Technology Planning

Associations must have a comprehensive technology plan for several reasons. First, the role of technology, particularly internet-based systems and platforms, will be increasingly critical to an association's relevance and performance. Secondly, the rate of technological advances will continue to accelerate. With these advances will come considerable growth in technological opportunities for associations, leading to difficult choices about what to adopt and how to allocate resources. Finally, the associated exposure to risk will increase. These conditions will be very unkind to an unprepared organization. A plan is required.

Only 42 percent of associations have a formal technology plan/strategy. (ASAE's *2006 Policies and Procedures*) Given that plans can be obsolete and that many aren't implemented, it could be argued that as few as 25 percent of associations are effectively guiding technology decision making with a plan. That more than half don't even have a plan confirms our assertion that associations have underestimated the impact and potential of technology. If they understood its critical role, they would know that a plan is necessary.

Start with the association's overall strategic plan. What are the priorities and the key result areas for the association? A primary role of your technology plan is to support the priorities in the strategic plan. How can you leverage technology to achieve your objectives?

The technology plan should also identify how technology can be used to improve organizational efficiency and productivity. While returns from technology investments can often be tricky to demonstrate, it would be difficult to argue that computers and software have not increased staff productivity.

Technology that strengthens the association's capacity to add value to current programs, services, and delivery mechanisms should be fully addressed. This is probably the largest area of catch up for most associations.

The technology plan should investigate opportunities to add value that were not previously possible. This requires maintaining awareness of technologies that have potential and a process to test them (which we address later in this chapter). Most of the technology improvements associations have made have been limited to transferring traditional programs or services to new technological delivery systems, like going from an ink-on-paper newsletter to an electronically delivered newsletter or converting traditional seminars into webinars. While laudable, true innovation has been lacking as associations have been hampered by the constraints of their paradigms. They are not thinking of what technology can do that was impossible in the past.

Online tradeshows demonstrate our point. The virtual tradeshows we have seen depict the traditional tradeshow set up: booths and aisles. The developers took what existed and moved it to the web. A more creative approach would have been to say, "The objective is to put buyer and seller together. What technologies exist or are being developed that could accomplish this access and interaction?"

The technology plan has to take into account the costs associated with maintaining the association's existing technology. This includes equipment upgrades, software updates, website hosting, internet service, and staff training and development.

Understanding the costs associated with maintaining and operating your current equipment, systems, and software is very important. If all you budget for is to continue your current technologies, you are going to fall behind. Maintenance and operating costs include software upgrades, equipment replacements, system updates, website hosting, service contracts, internet connection charges, security, virus protection, and more factors.

These costs can be considerable and if they are not anticipated and budgeted, there can be unfavorable consequences for your efforts to capitalize on new technology opportunities. If these expenses are under-estimated or inadequately budgeted, they will rob the funds for testing and developing new applications.

Resource Allocation

Associations are simply not allocating sufficient resources to tech-nology. The need for increased resource allocation has been growing for decades. One could argue that any organizational challenge or defi-ciency can be resolved with additional resources. But as we point out in Chapter Six, association resources are not well understood or directed to begin with. Once the commitment has been made to a technology-driven future, the search for resources can begin. Once the promise of technology is understood, judgments about resource reallocations will be facilitated. A clearer picture of where real return on investment will occur should emerge.

The Total Technology Spend

The total percentage of the typical association's annual budget allocated to technology is inadequate. Period. Most associations have been kidding themselves about what it takes.

According to ASAE's *Operating Ratio Report, 13th Edition* (2008), *(ORR)* the average spending by associations on technology, excluding staff, as a percentage of total annual budget is a *measly 1.6 percent.* This breaks down as follows:

Hardware	0.5 percent
Software	0.4 percent
Web Design	0.5 percent
Internet Service Provider	0.2 percent

The average association with a budget of $3.8 million (*2008 ORR*) has the equivalent of one full-time technology staff member. Further analysis of compensation for technology positions (Information Technology (IT) Chief, Network Engineer, Webmaster, Software Developer, Website Content Coordinator/Manager, and Database Administrator) indicates an average annual salary of $78,900 for all technology positions. (ASAE 2010 Compensation Study) Payroll "loads" of 30 percent would increase this to $102,570. (By payroll "loads" we mean additional costs such as workers comp, health insurance, retirement plans, Social Security and Medicare, which add to the actual salary expense.)

This means that a typical association with revenues of $4 million per year has a "technology spend" of $164,570 per year ($64,000 non-payroll and $102,570 payroll) or 4.1 percent of its annual budget.

Because associations vary significantly in size, structure, services, geography, and other factors, and because their levels of adopting technology differ, a one-size-fits all solution is folly. But you cannot play the "we're different" card—unless you want to lag behind when it comes to harnessing the power of technology for your association.

We propose two options for determining the level of increased spending on technology: (a) establishing a target based on a percentage of total revenue and/or (b) establishing a spending level equivalent to the association's budget for an activity or function with a comparable value.

Our research into analysis/ benchmarks on IT spending found considerable variation by industry on spending as a percentage of total revenue. And we also encountered debate on the appropriateness of using a revenue-to-spend ratio. According to Mark McDonald, an IT analyst, "We need to recognize that the metric has no meaning because the numerator does not influence the denominator. You might as well measure the weight of the board of directors and compare it to changes in sales—they have the same 'connective' logic between them."

But variation and validity aside, associations need some guidance. We'll go out on a limb for the sake of stimulating discussion and analysis and propose that associations should consider spending 7 to 8 percent of their total gross revenues on technology, including staff. This means that a "typical" association with $4 million in annual revenues should have a total technology spend of $280,000 to $320,000.

Use this proposed level for analysis and "what if" purposes. If your association did agree to fund IT at this level, what would it enable you to do? Would you know where to invest it? What gaps would you be able to fill? Would you simply be throwing money at IT? (Please don't. If this is the case, you should put the funds into reserves until you get a grip on how to invest in technology wisely.) Would you be able to demonstrate return for the investment?

The result of this dialogue may be to spend more or less than the 7 to 8 percent guideline. But the point is that the possibilities have been explored and that the potential has been given consideration.

The "equivalent" basis for the association's technology spend says, "We believe that our annual budget for a given functional area or expense has a return on investment that is comparable to the return we expect to receive from spending on technology.

So, let's set a budget for technology that is equal to what we spend in that area. For example, according to ASAE's *Operating Ratio Report, 13th Edition* (2008) average spending on "Volunteers/Governance/Boards/Committees" is 3.6 percent of total revenue. If your technology spend was significantly below this, you could set a budget allocating an equivalent amount to technology. "Meals provided at events" are 4.2 percent of the average associations total revenue. Again, if your spending is below that, couldn't you spend at least that on technology? Or you could combine "Postage and Shipping" at 1.7 percent with "Printing and Photocopying Costs" of 4.4 percent and arbitrarily set a technology spend at 6.1 percent. The underlying thinking is, "If we can spend it here, why couldn't we spend a comparable amount on technology?"

One could certainly argue (and someone will) that the above is comparing apples to oranges, and that is true. But what we are trying to generate with this approach is some thought and discussion, not a cookie-cutter solution or an inflexible formula designed to set spending levels.

The Payout

Why the increased spending on technology? What is the return on investment? Associations should expect the following results:

- The ability to deliver information and communications in the way members increasingly prefer to receive it;

- The relevance to the next generation of members who are highly likely to accelerate their use of technology;

- The capacity to overcome time and distance barriers to participation and utilization;

- The capability to add value not possible with traditional delivery vehicles; and

- The opportunity to achieve improvements in productivity and efficiency.

Where Is the Money Going to Come From?

Meeting the targeted "technology spend" will not be easy, but the more rigorous approach to program costs proposed in Chapter Six will be a major help. There are four areas where you can make major inroads:

1. Redirect Contributions to Reserves. Given the role of technology in the effective association of the future, we believe technology investments are far more important than building reserves. The first step is to redirect a portion of contributions from the reserve fund to your technology budgets, staff, or systems.

It is a simple question. Let's say the association typically contributes $50,000 annually to the reserve fund. The leaders of this association simply have to ask, "What would we rather have in three years, another $150,000 in the bank or a portion of that dedicated to significantly improved technological capabilities?"

2. Redirect Subsidies. The evaluation of the costs associated with developing, delivering, and maintaining each of an association's programs and services is going to illuminate fee-for-service programs that cost more to produce than they generate in revenue. As a result, they require subsidies from dues or profitable programs to operate. As you eliminate these programs, you can free up the subsidies they require and redirect them to your technology spending.

3. Draw Down Reserves. First, most associations have no idea of what they will use their reserve funds for. We mentioned earlier in this chapter the lack of written policies or guidelines that would direct the use of reserves. Second, the need to use reserves doesn't happen frequently. As Steve Gennett, CEO of Carolinas Associated General Contractors, Inc., says in the case study at the end of this chapter, "I have been in this business for 43 years. I can't even count on three fingers the number of times that we had a significant stress in the operation where we had to say, 'Well, we've got reserves to back this up.'" Many associations curiously accumulate reserves to reach a level equal to one year's operating costs, which makes no sense if you think about it. We put this money aside in the event that if we have no income whatsoever, we can run the association for one more year? Like a victory lap?

Second, it could be argued that the association's lagging position in technology constitutes a "rainy day" and that tapping reserves is appropriate. This argument is most valid in the case of an association's need to catch up.

4. Increase Revenue. If technology enhancements have, in fact, added value, shouldn't an increase in dues capture that value? Though it won't likely happen in the short term, eventually the association's technology investments should represent revenue-generating opportunities.

Getting to the necessary level of technology spending is not going to be easy. It will require tough choices. It will likely require a combination of all four of the above sources and should be incorporated into the association's strategic and technology multi-year plans.

Risk Taking: Testing

Associations have never been expected to be risk takers. For the most part, they didn't have to be. Today's complex and fast-moving technological environment requires risk taking. It cannot be avoided. The comprehensive technology plan is the first step in improving risk-taking approaches. The plan will include an assessment of the association's technological status; an analysis of the technological environment and opportunities; technological assumptions; and options, priorities, and resource requirements. The process will identify risks and the exposures or opportunities involved.

Another key strategy to deal with technology's uncertainty and risks is a system that includes small-scale testing of emerging technologies.

An association could categorize or sort its technology efforts into four groups:

- Necessary maintenance and upgrades;
- Technologies in the process of full development;
- Technologies not to be pursued; and
- Emerging technologies that should be tested.

The test is a limited trial of a technology. Tests should be used when a technology's relevance or efficacy are unknown. The objective of a test is to reduce the risk of fully investing in a technology that may or may not perform. Clay Shirky said it well: "You need the ability to try several small things at once. Then you can say, 'Those aren't working, let's stop.' And 'These are working, let's keep going.' And for the stuff in the middle, 'Can we try for another angle on this?'" (*Associations Now*, Feb. 2010).

For tests to work, they must be initiated early in the technology's life cycle. You have to catch them early, so that if they prove to have potential, you can capitalize on them as their impact or utility is at its optimum. If you test too late in the life cycle, you may be in the position of full deployment when the technology is maturing, competition is increasing, or the technology is going into decline. Early identification of technology opportunities requires diligence in scanning media for news of introductions or advances. Your association will need an organized and ongoing scanning process to feed your testing program.

Another key to successful testing is managing expectations. A test is, by design, on a small scale. When evaluating results, the association must keep in mind that the technology's performance is likely to be on a small scale as well. The best approach is to carefully define success before the test is initiated. To consider this test a success, what should we expect and in what time frame should it occur?

For example, let's say that in the fall of 2003 you decided to test a group on LinkedIn (launched in May 2003). The professional networking site looked interesting and would be an enhancement to the association's existing listserver. Your test is limited to a single special interest group of 40 members currently using the listserver. You define success as getting 20 of these members to convert to the LinkedIn group within 30 days. If that works, you will expand the effort to move three more interest groups over to LinkedIn in the next 60 days.

In this same scenario, a little more aggressive test might have been to simultaneously try to convert another listserver interest group to MySpace (also launched in 2003). You could then compare results and determine which social networking vehicle worked best.

In the last 10 years, many technologies would have lent themselves to testing: electronic newsletters, online directories, blogs, webinars, and other things.

The testing approach has a good deal of potential for associations as the rate of technological advances increase in the future. But you need to be quick and decisive. You need to be willing to drop unsuccessful tests and not let them linger. You may need to even retest in instances when your test was premature. But testing will get you in the game and keep your risks in check.

Technology Options Matrix

As with member segmentation and the product and service mix, a matrix can help you identify technology areas to watch, test, and acquire for your association. The numerical assessment is intended to generate objective thinking in assessing the factors important to technology decisions. The "forced choice" approach eliminates the tendency to give high ratings across the board.

The directions for using this matrix, shown on the next page, are the same as in previous chapters:

List all technology options in the first vertical column. All types of possible technologies should be listed: new/upgrades; large/small opportunities; hardware/software; Internet-based, whatever other options are being used or considered.

Total the number of all options. Divide the total by 5 for your "rating quota." For example, if you have 25 technology opportunities listed, you

Technology Options	Relevance to strategic plan priorities	Capacity to add new value to membership	Ability to enhance delivery of value	Financial impact	Improved efficiencies or productivity	Impact on how the association is perceived	Required to maintain current capabilities	Level of risk	Total Priority Rating

divide by 5 and your rating quota is 5. The quota limits the number of options you can give high rankings, and forces you to give lower rankings.

Under each vertical column heading, you should assign a number from 1 to 5 to each option. A "5" is the highest or most favorable rating and a "1" the lowest. However, you must assign ratings limited by your rating quota. In the example above with 25 technology options, you can give only five options a "5" rating, five options a "4" rating and so on. (Yes, five options must be given a "1.") We recommend that you fill in your five "5s" first, then the five "1s." Then go back and fill in your five "4s," then the five "2s," and the five "3s."

Total the ratings horizontally and rank them from the highest total to the lowest.

Use the rankings to make judgments about your association's technology priorities and allocations from your technology spend.

Questions to Initiate Dialogue

Use the matrix to begin your efforts to place the appropriate emphasis on technological opportunities and facilitate the discussion by posing the following questions:

- Are we paying adequate attention to the growing potential of information and communication technologies to add value to membership?

- Is it a good assumption that technological advances will accelerate and have an increasing impact on how the association does business and delivers value?

- Are our members ahead of us in adopting technology? (For example, who showed up at a meeting with the first Blackberry or iPhone, a volunteer or staff member?) If our members are ahead of us, what percentage would you estimate are adopting technology faster than the association is?

- What is the condition of our technology infrastructure? Has it been maintained and upgraded appropriately?

- What percentage of our budget is allocated to maintenance, testing, and development of our information and communication technologies?

- Do we have a current organization-wide plan for technology (including paying for continuing education in order to learn about emerging technologies)? If so, is it being followed?

- Do we have adequate staff (size and expertise) to ensure we're keeping up with the rapid advances in technology?

- Would we benefit from partnering long-term with a technology consultant to supplement current staff or provide the expertise unavailable on staff?

Summary

Lack of expertise, intimidation, expense, and the speed and scale with which technology is changing are the main reasons many associations are lagging behind when it comes to technology. Though these obstacles are formidable, they are not insurmountable, especially when an association has both a strategic plan and a three-year technology plan. With careful planning and wise and regular spending, it is possible for today's association to keep pace with the rapidly changing technological landscape. We hope we've made a strong argument that doing so is no longer a luxury. It's a necessity. The race is on.

Radical Change: Harnessing the Power of Technology

ASSOCIATION: Carolinas Associated General Contractors, Inc. (CAGC)

BUDGET: $8,000,000

NUMBER OF STAFF MEMBERS: 57

NUMBER OF MEMBERS: 3,000

CASE STUDY:

For decades, Carolinas Associated General Contractors, Inc. (CAGC) produced printed bulletins with information about projects for member contractors to bid on. Approximately 14 years ago, the association launched a project to deliver construction plans and specifications in a CD format. Members could subscribe to a special edition in which project plans were included on the disk as a bonus. Despite its best efforts, CAGC built the subscription list up to 80 members, but it needed 120 to break even. After 18 months and an investment of nearly $250,000, the association abandoned the project.

As it did for most associations, the emergence of the internet changed everything. A staff member convinced Steve Gennett, CEO, that the internet provided the platform necessary to transform how the association delivered information about bidding projects. Though CAGC had failed with the CDs, the association partnered with a vendor to provide bidding data online, a much more efficient way to disseminate the information to members.

When it became clear that the vendor wasn't open to functionality changes and improvements suggested by members, staff began discussing the possibility of developing proprietary software to meet member needs. The projected cost of doing so was $1.2 million. In spite of the previous failure, staff approached leadership with the idea and got permission to borrow start-up funds. To reduce risk, CAGC approached two other state chapters and invited them to join the effort. Each chapter would contribute $400,000 and equally share the profits. Though one group expressed interest, both ultimately opted not to participate, citing the cost. CAGC was on its own.

The entrepreneurial culture of the association made it possible to take a big risk and consequently enjoy great reward. Notes Gennett, "I think about looking at your operation more in terms of it functioning in a business context, rather than an association management context…. I also think the staff has to be made to understand that they are to be creative in their work, since all new ideas may not come from a committee." Approaching volunteer leadership with a detailed businesslike proposal enabled the association to meet member needs directly and profitably.

Though many associations view their reserve funds as untouchable, thus limiting their potential to finance development of beneficial member services, the commitment to funding the project came from CAGC's reserves. Gennett says, "I think associations overplay the reserve dollars in terms of funding that has to be built up and maintained. I have been in this business for 43 years. I can't even count on three fingers the number of times that we had a significant stress in the operation where we had to say, "Well, we've got reserves to back this up." In addition, he says, "I look at reserves as much as anything else as a research and development fund."

Today, 800 firms pay $1,995 each to subscribe to IBuild, producing annual revenue of $1.6 million. Initial conservative projections indicated the project would reach profitability in five to six years. Yet the launch of IBuild was so successful that CAGC paid off the loan in just three years.

The transition from long-time dependency on a paper bulletin to internet-delivered information was a challenge. Initially, 230 firms (mostly smaller ones struggling to keep up with technology) dropped their membership after the online service began and the paper format was discontinued. Many have since returned, but it was a bold move to alienate so many members at the beginning of the project.

In addition to revenue, having complete ownership of IBuild produced an unexpected dividend for CAGC. Before it owned the software, any time the organization wanted to change its functionality, it had to sell the idea to its partnering vendor. Now, when a member calls with a suggestion or request for a change, staff can respond quickly. Gennett says, "There are times when we've been able to have functionality developed and operating within 24 hours" in response to a member suggestion. That's the power of technology—and the beauty of harnessing it to help members be more successful in their own businesses.

Radical Change: Staying Ahead of Your Members

ASSOCIATION: Texas Trial Lawyers Association's separate company called TrialSmith®

TRIALSMITH® ANNUAL REVENUE: $3.3 million

NUMBER OF TRIALSMITH® STAFF MEMBERS: 16 full-time equivalents

NUMBER OF TRIALSMITH® PARTICIPANTS: 85,000

CASE STUDY:

Though Tommy Townsend, CAE, executive director of the Texas Trial Lawyers Association (TTLA), didn't grow up with a computer, email or the internet, he knew it was going to take the association world by storm. "It was apparent to me that the whole technology thing was going to sweep over everything. And I knew I didn't know enough about it to really address it," he says. So he did what any smart manager would do: He searched for the most talented, knowledgeable technology person he could find—and hired Kent Hughes, CAE.

Hughes' first job was simply to get TTLA up to speed with the hardware necessary to take advantage of emerging technology. Then he, Townsend, and a couple of innovative past presidents of the Texas Trial Lawyers Association began talking about "the next thing they could do through technology to provide a member service." As a result, in 1997, DepoConnect, an online database of depositions, was born. Townsend recalls, "A lawyer would call another and say, 'I remember you had a case with so-and-so as an expert. Did you take his deposition? If so, would you mail it to me?' There was a huge volume of mail going back and forth."

Townsend and his team automated the effort, a move so popular that other trial lawyer associations asked for access. Today, more than 468,000 depositions are online. As other states joined DepoConnect, money rolled in. "We had to do something internally because we were beginning to make too much money," remembers Townsend. Renamed TrialSmith®, DepoConnect became a for-profit subsidiary—and the growth continued.

Listservers were the next frontier; today the organization hosts 500 list-servers with a volume of more than 2.5 million emails per day. Then along came developing websites and hosting sites for 109 associations (not all trial-lawyer specific).

As TrialSmith® grew, the popularity of the program led to an affinity agreement in which trial lawyer associations earn a rebate composed of a percentage of the services used by their respective members. In 2009, more than 128 associations and litigation groups received rebates totaling $592,000 from TrialSmith® and its distance learning division, SeminarWeb.

In 2000, revenues dictated that operations move from a for-profit subsidiary to a for-profit corporation. Though TTLA is the majority stockholder, the association currently does not take any money from the company other than the percentage earned through its rebate, similar to other affiliated associations. Revenue for TTLA from TrialSmith® in 2009 totaled $26,400.

Innovation continues to be the name of the game at TrialSmith®, which offers EClips, a clipping service that assembles and delivers daily news from a variety of sources via email each morning; JurySmith, a service that provides background via almost instant reports about potential jurors compiled from public records to help with jury selection; and Justice Nation, a social network for trial lawyers, allowing them to easily connect with other attorneys.

TrialSmith® lawyers now number over 85,000—and all are members of a trial lawyers association, since membership at some level is required to participate. Subscription rates range from $179 (access only to the listservers and FastCase Law Library) to $1,099 for a firm subscription, which includes all TrialSmith® services.

The rapid growth of TrialSmith® is due not only to the vision and know-how of Kent Hughes but also to leadership who embraced the concept of developing technology as a member benefit. Notes Townsend, "They ran interference for us with some doubters within our association because we invested a lot of money in it to start it up. It's so critical that you have a partnership with enlightened leadership." And he reiterates the need for the skilled knowledge similar to what Kent Hughes continues to offer TrialSmith® as its president. Says Townsend, "Hire the best people you can and remove any barriers. And be prepared to take risk."

CHAPTER EIGHT

Strategies for Success

We said it earlier, but it warrants being repeated: The change to a five-member competency-based board comes first. Tackling the remaining changes will be far less formidable and the prospects of success go up by a factor of 100 with the small, carefully selected board.

It is no coincidence that in *Good to Great,* Jim Collins identifies the importance of "getting the right people on the bus" to achieve greatness as an organization. In this context, we are emphasizing getting the right people in the driver's seat. Radically changing your thinking about the member market, your product line, and technology is not an easy road to travel. You need a small group of thoughtfully selected leaders to steer your organization to its preferred future. An analogy would be a sailing ship, with the board positioned in the crow's nest giving direction and with the CEO at the rudder. Staying with the nautical metaphor, too many boards are below the deck at the oars on a Roman trireme, pulling on the three rows of oars on each side.

Now that you know the scale of the other proposed radical changes, you have a better appreciation of why a well-composed, small board is important, if not essential, for success.

Your best argument for the five-member board is that it exists today, de facto. Almost all associations, regardless of board size, really operate at the direction of an executive committee or group of officers. Why don't more associations just formalize what is already a common practice?

The sequence of the other changes is important as well. You can't right-size your product and service lines until you have critically evaluated and decided on the member market. And you can't make decisions on technology until you know what you are going to deliver. The best way to proceed is one step at a time, with each step building on the last.

But what if you're not able to accomplish the first step by moving to a five-member competency-based board? There are some cases where it's not possible. Move on to the next steps and accomplish the changes one at a time. Your organization will still benefit from an empowered CEO and enhanced staff, a clearly defined member market, a narrow program and service offering, and a robust technology framework.

Keystone Questions

Thought-provoking, probing, sometimes uncomfortable questions may be the best way to initiate important dialogue about radical change. Once you have a small, competency-based board in place, such questions will become even more valuable. The previous chapters pose sets of questions to raise consciousness regarding various aspects of radical change. These are a good start. Your circumstances likely will require that you add, delete, or modify questions to best fit your association's situation. As a reminder, here's a sampling:

- What major industry or professional changes or trends have resulted in changes in the profile (size, scope, operating model, etc.) of the member?

- What would segmentation of the member market reveal if you compared 1960 to 2010?

- What membership segments have high nonrenewal rates? Why?

- What potential membership segments are more difficult to recruit? Who are "hard sells" in your recruitment campaigns? Why?

- Are you allocating resources to focus on opportunities to add value?

- Knowing what you know today, what extensions of the member market undertaken by the association in the past did not produce the anticipated results? If you could turn the clock back and remake the decision, would you? Why?

- Do you allocate resources primarily based on history and tradition or based on tomorrow's opportunities?

- Which services or activities failed to measure up to expectations, particularly after several attempts to promote them more effectively? Which services have "taken off" and are more successful than you thought they would be?

- Are you paying adequate attention to the growing potential of information and communication technologies to add value to membership?

- What is the condition of your technology infrastructure? Has it been maintained and upgraded appropriately?

- Are you allocating resources to what you know how to do versus what you should be doing?

- Are you allocating sufficient resources to the development and testing of new programs, services, and delivery mechanisms?

- Where are resources being allocated with marginal return?

When crafting your questions, keep in mind the objectives. First, you want to bring attention to the issue. Give it the appropriate emphasis and urgency. Get it "on the table." Many times the issue has been skirted. Addressing it openly has been uncomfortable for a variety of reasons. Often it has been discussed informally but not in board or executive committee meetings. In many cases, once it has been breached, someone will comment, "I've often wondered why this hasn't come up for discussion before."

If you are an association staff professional, consider sharing this book with your board and/or selected leaders and staff, then discussing it. (We can't help mentioning that multiple copies are available at a discount through ASAE.) We've written it for the purpose of stimulating both thought and discussion, recognizing that radical change requires new thinking. We've shared what we hope are new and challenging ideas as well as what other organizations are doing in hopes of encouraging you and your leaders to adapt what you've read for your own organization.

Second, frame the issue. Size the scale of the issue. Explore the potential or consequences. Stimulate an assessment that will lead to action one way or the other. During the course of the subsequent dialogue and analysis, the issue will "take" and the need to address it will be recognized. Or there may be cases when action may not be seen as appropriate. In other situations, leadership may dodge or dismiss the discussion. One way or another, you have gained valuable intelligence and you are better informed than when you started the discussion.

The Importance of Data

One outcome from posing the keystone questions may be that the association doesn't have the answers and you'll see that data is lacking.

To make radical changes in an association, you must have data to support your case. You must be armed with sound information. Without the facts, your chances of success are virtually nonexistent.

Associations have very strong, deeply ingrained cultures. They have profound, long-standing traditions. They have powerful and intricate political dynamics. They are manipulated by influential and formidable personalities, including, in many cases, a bank of opinionated past presidents. They often value the status quo. Most are reactive rather than proactive. Quite frankly, most associations are hostile environments for change.

In the association environment, you don't stand much of a chance of making a case without data. But the facts can be a powerful strategic resource in promulgating change, particularly radical change.

Don't even try without data. For the most part, the information is accessible. You may not capture it in the format that you need, but with a little work you can get it. Here are some thoughts to help you put your facts together:

Don't get overwhelmed. In some cases there may be considerable data voids and filling them in may look like an insurmountable task. It will require time and taxing work, but get on it. You aren't going very far, if anywhere, without it.

If your data voids are considerable, prioritize and get to work. Pick the information that will be most compelling. Identify the facts that will be difficult, if not impossible, to argue against. What key piece of data will be most convincing in making your point?

Concentrate data gathering in a short, specific time frame. Set aside two days, lock staff in a room, turn off the smart phones, and don't let them out until they crunch the numbers. Let's face it; compiling statistics has little sex appeal for most people. As a result, it will always be put off. Use a time-specific deadline to get it done. It is your most important ammunition. You can't go to battle without it.

When the perfect data is not available, use the best you have.
Let's say that you don't have comprehensive retention rates by member segments. Go with the best you can compile, like retention rates of a sample of the member segment. You can use good, sound estimates. The statistics may not be airtight, but they can be defensible. And they can be effective, particularly when your opponents don't have anything but emotional appeals or vague assumptions to support their positions.

Use the Matrix

The matrix could be your best friend in the change process.

Having the data is critical, but the matrix translates it to a format that is an easy-to-understand, comprehensive analysis of the issue you are addressing. It provides you and your leadership a thorough "snapshot" of the issue, analyzing and organizing the data to facilitate decision making.

The matrix concept emerged from our observations of association leadership and staff wrestling with tough decisions. Most of the debate was based on subjective positions, personal experience or perspectives, politically motivated viewpoints, or unsubstantiated assumptions and input that start with the words, "I think…." Not a pretty picture. Numerical ratings were our way of forcing objectivity into the equation. "Objective" is defined as "uninfluenced by emotions or personal prejudices; based on observable phenomena; presented factually." Associations need a tool or technique to get there. Thus, the matrix. By setting aside rhetoric and putting a relative priority or weight to each list of options using a forced choice numerical system, you'll have a better chance of guiding your leadership team to truly objective decisions.

Another problem we have encountered is decision making on single issues without regard for context. There is nothing strategic about piecemeal decision making. Resources should not be allocated without consideration of options or the consequences on current or future efforts. Adding a service without considering everything else you are doing or have planned is unwise. Deciding to adopt a new technology application without considering what is currently in place or in the works is short-sighted. The matrix encourages you to look at the whole picture by making services compete with one another, or technologies compete for resources, or member segments compete for support. Good decisions aren't made in isolation. The matrix makes you consider the full context. It may not necessarily result in an easier decision, but certainly a better one.

The forced choice feature of our matrices design is essential. All of us have been in sessions where groups rate everything "high priority" or "most important." The forced choice model imposes a discipline on the analysis process. It requires your team to make judgments and differentiate between options.

Caution: People are apt to balk at making the choices. We have seen groups spend inordinate time agonizing over a single rating on a matrix. They wring their hands. They scratch their heads. They moan and groan. "Is this a 3 or a 4? I just don't know." Sometimes this behavior is a reflection of the challenge in making decisions. Other times it is simply a dodge. They know the answer; they just don't want to face up to it.

Our recommendations for completing a matrix follow:

Take time to ensure that the rating factors (those on the horizontal) are appropriate for your association. We have provided a good start, but almost all of our templates require some tailoring to fit an association's unique situation or priorities. To download free copies of the templates in this book, go to www.raceforrelevance.com.

Assemble all the data available before you start. Pull together financial information, survey results, and whatever other information is required in advance. Make sure it is organized so that it can be easily factored into the matrix ratings.

Select the right people to complete the matrix. These should be people who are familiar with the issues/services being analyzed. It may be staff. It may be volunteers aided by staff. At the minimum, it should be one or more people with knowledge about the items listed on the matrix: usage rates, associated costs, and other factors.

Convene a time-limited session. Give respondents 90 minutes to develop the first draft. Completing a matrix before a strategic planning session can provide the planning group with a valuable resource to be incorporated into their decision making.

Convert the ratings from the matrix to an Excel spreadsheet and reconvene the group for a review to make appropriate revisions. Once the Excel formulas have been set, you can change ratings and recalculate easily.

Quick Wins

In his 1996 book, *Leading Change*, John P. Kotter recommends creating "short-term wins." These victories early in the change process fuel the appetite for continued pursuit of the longer-term objective.

With each change, you should identify specific opportunities to demonstrate that changes are producing results and that the effort is working. Communicating these early wins will keep your critics at bay and provide encouragement to your team. Pick short-term targets that are achievable, quantifiable, and are highly unlikely to fail. The best candidates are "no brainers" that you are certain you will achieve.

For example, what expense reductions did you realize with a smaller board? What new member recruits did you make in the member market as now defined? What were the increases in member participation in the activities where you are concentrating your resources? What member utilization are you experiencing on a newly adopted technology? Make sure that these are communicated quickly and effectively to both staff and appropriate leadership.

Burn Your Bridges

There is an old admonishment that one should never "burn his bridges." The thinking is that once you cross a bridge and burn it, you will not have the option of going back that way.

Once a radical change has been implemented, we encourage you to do just the opposite: Burn the bridge so that you cannot regress to the previous structure or practices.

You can burn bridges in different ways. Make a change in the bylaws that institutionalizes the change. Establish a policy that makes regression difficult if not impossible. Design procedures that cement the change in place.

In 1519, Spanish Conquistador Hernando Cortez landed on the shores of Mexico with the goal of seizing the treasures of the Aztecs. Before leading his men into battle, he instructed them to burn 11 of the ships on which they had arrived. Now defeat was not an option. There was only one course. If they were going to survive, they would have to be committed to victory.

By burning your bridges—or your ship—you'll ensure that your organization is on the move, rather than staying stuck in the past or the comfort of today.

Preparing for the Adventure

Radical change is not without risk. Though we've personally seen that the risk is worth the reward of creating a relevant, thriving association that operates with an eye toward excellence now while proactively looking to the future, there are potential hazards. Forcing change against the complacency of your membership can create divisions and distrust. Wrangling over how to make changes can result in gridlock and stalemates or further heighten differences of opinion between volunteer leaders. Changing for change's sake without a thorough understanding of why you're doing it can wreak havoc. And, frankly, if you push too hard, it's possible to jeopardize your job and/or alienate the leadership team (both staff and volunteer) you work with.

The association executives we interviewed who have initiated the radical changes we've discussed have several things in common. Their experiences will be helpful to you as you lead your association to relevance. Keep these in mind and you'll experience smoother sailing as you affect radical change within your organization.

Don't run alone. Change leaders realize the course is much more difficult if they are on it alone. Get support first from a couple of leaders you are close to, whom you respect, and whom others respect as well. Then, let them help you set the pace in the race for relevance.

Recognize that doing nothing is not an option. Those who lead radical change realize that maintaining the status quo is not an option. As soon as they complete one change, they begin looking for another. This keeps their leaders on their toes and looking ahead as well. It also makes it difficult for micromanagement to occur when the scale of change is radical and the pace is rapid.

Have a crystal-clear vision and specific destination. You don't need to know how the vision is going to be realized when you begin the change process, but you do need to be able to describe it clearly to staff, leaders, and any partners you'll be working with to create change. The more clearly you see the finish line, the more likely you'll be able to reach it.

Focus on the reward. Being a change agent is not for the faint of heart. It takes courage, creativity, and persistence. You will be criticized, vilified, and second-guessed. The course may be long and you may experience hurdles along the way. Focus on the benefit of the change to keep you going even when you encounter obstacles or when fatigue temporarily saps your energy.

Make course adjustments as necessary. Some impediments will remain hidden until your efforts are well underway. Don't be discouraged when you run into them. In other cases, your results may exceed your expectations and you may catch a second wind and get ahead of the plan. In both instances, make appropriate course corrections and keep moving forward.

Communicate, communicate, and communicate. Then communicate more. Repetition is the mother of all learning—and the mother of all remembering. It's your job to cast a vision and remind your team why you're undertaking radical change in the first place. Paint a picture of an association with vitality and energy that volunteer leadership and staff want to be a part of. Doing so will keep everyone moving forward.

The Radical Change Artist of Today

We started this journey together by recognizing the challenges facing today's associations: loss of market share, increased competition for members' time, shrinking revenue sources, rapid advances in technology, higher member expectations, increased competition, and more diverse member markets.

Throughout this book we've looked at a variety of fundamental changes: how to lead, manage, and think about our organizations; how we should look at member markets; and how we might structure and deliver programs and services. And we've equipped you with questions, matrices, and tactics for leading your organization through radical change. For more, join us at www.raceforrelevance.com.

The associations that have relevance in the future will be those that tackle the tough questions and decisions today—leading to radical change tomorrow. They need courageous and creative risk-takers leading the race in order to prosper. The rewards are worth it. We've seen it time and time again in the associations we work with. Hard work now will ensure your organization is poised for the future and will thrive—not just survive.

Acknowledgements

The authors would like to thank

Rick Alampi

John Albers

Stephanie Blodig

Gary Bolinger, CAE

Rebecca Brandt, CAE

Karen Conner

Harm J. de Blij, Ph.D.

Chip Deale

Monica Dignam

Douglas Ducate, CEM, CMP

Mike Fisher

Sandra Fisher

Mike Garcia

Steve Gennett

Donna Harman

Kent Hughes, CAE

Gary LaBranche, CAE

Dave Lukens

Lori Maarschalk

Jill Martineau Cornish, IOM

Nancy Matthes, CAE

Tiffany McGee

Shawn Montgomery, MLS

Scott Norvell

Marcia Poell Holston

Robert Prall

J. Clarke Price, CAE

Linda Raynes

Maria Saino

Steve Sandherr

Juliet Shor

Alex Siegel

Keith Skillman, CAE

Barbara Thompson

Tommy Townsend

Joseph P. Truncale, CAE

Baron Williams, CAE

Suggested Readings

ASAE Publications

- Dalton, James, and Dignam, Monica. *The Decision to Join: How Individuals Determine Value and Why They Choose to Belong.* ASAE, 2007.

- *Operating Ratio Report, 13th Edition.* ASAE, 2008.

- *Policies and Procedures in Association Management: A Benchmarking Guide.* ASAE, 2006.

Books

- Collins, J. *Good to Great: Why Some Companies Make the Leap...and Others Don't.* Harper Business Press, 2001.

- Drucker, P. *Management: Tasks, Responsibilities, Practices.* Harper Paperbacks, 1993.

- Harari, O. *Leapfrogging the Competition: Five Giant Steps to Becoming a Market Leader, 2nd Edition.* Prima Lifestyles, 1999.

- Kotter, J. *Leading Change.* Harvard Business Press, 1996.

- Lencioni, P. *The Five Dysfunctions of a Team: A Leadership Fable.* Jossey-Bass, 2002.

- Porter, M. *Competitive Strategy: Techniques for Analyzing Industries and Competition.* Free Press, 1998.

- Rogers, E. *Diffusion of Innovations, 5th Edition.* Free Press, 2003.

- Wilcox, P. *Exposing the Elephants: Creating Exceptional Nonprofits.* Wiley, 2006.

Index

A

AAHA, *see* American Animal Hospital
Association
Activities offered by associations, *see*
Programs offered by associations, *see also*
Services offered by associations
AFPA, *see* American Forest and Paper
Association
AGCA, *see* Associated General Contractors
of America
Alampi, Rick, 43
Albers, John, 45
AMA, *see* American Medical Association
American Animal Hospital Association
(AAHA), 45–46
Leadership Identification Committee, 45
American Forest and Paper Association
(AFPA), 77–78
American Medical Association (AMA),
77–78
American Society of Association Executives
(ASAE)
*Association Compensation and Benefits
Study, 2008/2009 Edition,* 68
1996 Policies and Procedures, 68
*2006 ASAE Policies and Procedures
in Association Management:
A Benchmarking Guide,* 104–105
Operating Ratio Report, 13th Edition,
(2008), 104
2010 Compensation and Benefits Study, 68
Andrews, Kenneth, 15
ASAE, *see* American Society of Association
Executives

Associated General Contractors of America
(AGCA), 115–116
Association of Junior Leagues International, 8

B

Baby boomers, 15, 17, *see also* Trends
affecting association membership
Board composition
committees and, 47, 53
constituencies, 28–29
downsizing, 38–39
small, competency-based boards, 32–37
special interests, 28–29
Board functioning, 26–27
chief executive officer and, 63–64, 65
election of directors, 29
executive committee, 27–28
relationship with staff, 64–65
responsibilities, 63
size of, 27–28, 29
terms of members, 28, 29
Bolinger, CAE, Gary, 36

C

CAGC, *see* Carolinas Associated General
Contractors, Inc.
Carey, CAE, Stephen, 13
Carolinas Associated General Contractors,
Inc. (CAGC), 139–140
CEIR, *see* Center for Exhibition Industry
Research
Center for Exhibition Industry Research
(CEIR), 19
Change in associations, approaches to, 3–4, 5
implementing, 145–146

information collection, 146–147
matrix, use of, 147–149
questions to ask, 144–145
risks taking within, 150–152
Chief Executive Officer, 63–64
expertise, 66
Collins, Jim, 4, 69, 100, 143, *see also* Good to
Great
Committees, 47
changes in, 50–51
dynamics in, 49–50
education, 59
executive, 58–59
management of, 52–53
overhauling, 54–55
staff involvement, 57–58
volunteers, 48, 50, 51–52, 57–58
Compensation and benefits for executives
and staff, 68–69
Competency-based boards, 32
board qualifications, 36
chief executive officer, 57, 66–67
communication, 62–63
consultant, use of, 59–60
director screening process, 32–33
downsizing, 38–39
governance test, 33–34
implementing change to, 37–39, 40,
41–42
safeguards, 37–38
selection of five directors, 34–36, 37–38
staff qualifications, 37, 66
staff trends, 57–58
troubleshooting member response to
change, 40–42
volunteer involvement, 57–58, 67
Competitive Strategy, 99
Conference preparation, 60–61
old vs. new methods, 61–62
Consolidation, as it affects the member
market, 79
Crowe, David, 12

D
de Blij, Ph.D., Harm J., 153
Decision to Join, The, 10, 16–17
Decision to Volunteer, The, 31
Diffusion of Innovations, 123
Directors of boards, 31
elections of, 28–29
qualifications of, 34–35
reasons to be, 31–32
Downsizing, 38–39, 40–41

Drucker, Peter F., 99, 107
Ducate, Douglas L., 19

E
EASA, *see* Electrical Apparatus Service
Association
80/20 rule, *see* Pareto Principle
Electrical Apparatus Service Association
(EASA), 71
theory and design models, 72

F
Facebook, 22
Five Dysfunctions of a Team, The, 62
Full-service association, 105–106
vs. narrow-service association, 106

G
Garcia, Mike, 153
Generation X, 15–16, 17, 19–20, *see also*
Trends affecting association membership
Gennett, CEO, Steve, 139, 140
Geographic composition of board, 28
G.I. Generation, 15, *see also* Trends affecting
association membership
Globalization, 76–77
Good to Great, 69, 100, 143
Hedgehog Concept, 100

H
Hackman, Richard, 32
Harari, Oren, 99
Hughes, CAE, Kent, 141, 142

I-J
Information delivery models,
internet, v
Innovation diffusion, 123
International Congress and Convention
Association, 96–97

K
Kotter, John P., 149

L
Lang, CPA, Andrew, 101
Leading Change, 149
Lencioni, Patrick, 62
Levin, CAE, CSP, Mark, 96
Low, Jim (ASAE), 11
Lukens, Dave, 115, 116

M

Management: Tasks, Responsibilities, and Practices, 107
Management styles, vi
    changes to be made, 3, 5
Master Builders of Iowa (MBI), 117–118
MBI, *see* Master Builders of Iowa
McGee, Tiffany, 90–91
Member market,
    affiliate or associate, 81–82
    changing the, 86–89
    consolidation and, 79
    defining, 84–86
    evaluating, 86–89
    expectations, 1–2, 9, 79, 83
    growth of, 81
    limiting, 83–84
    multiple constituencies, 80
    relevance matrix, 87
    return on investment, 10–11, 80
Members
    board governance, 26–27
    recruitment, 82–83
Membership,
    decline, 2–3
    trends influencing, *see* Trends affecting association membership
Millennials, 15–16, 19–20, 22, *see also* Trends affecting association membership

N

National Association for Printing Leadership, 92
National Association of Home Builders, 12
National Automobile Dealers Association, 13
New Jersey Veterinary Medical Association (NJVMA), 43–44
NJVMA, *see* New Jersey Veterinary Medical Association
Norvell, Scott, 117–118
Nour, David, 122

O

Ohio Society of Certified Public Accountants (OSCPA), 73
    Clark Price, CAE, and, 73
Operating models, 1
    trends affecting, 3, *see also* Trends affecting association membership
OSCPA, *see* Ohio Society of Certified Public Accountants

P-Q

Pareto Principle, 95
Planning tools, vii–viii
Porter, Michael, 99
Pozen, Richard, 32
Programs offered by associations, 97, *see* Services offered by associations
    chief executive officer and implementation of, 97–98
    committee involvement, 98
    concentrating resources to provide, 99
    membership influence, 98
    "profitability," 101
    resource allocations, 100–101
        analyzing, 103
        human, 101
        intangible, 102
    risk-free rationale, 109
    staff involvement, 98

R

Raynes, Linda, 153
Rogers, Everett, 123

S

Sandusky, Vince, 18
Services offered by associations, 96, *see also* Programs offered by associations
    communicating with members about, 106–108
    evaluating current, 109–110
        gathering information, 111–112
        program and service evaluation matrix, 112–114
    simplifying, 108
Sheet Metal and Air Conditioning Contractors' National Association (SMACNA), 18
Shirky, Clay, 134
Silents, 15–16, *see also* Trends affecting association membership
Sirk, CEO, Martin, 96–97
Sladek, Sarah, 17–18
SMACNA, *see* Sheet Metal and Air Conditioning Contractors' National Association
Social loafing, 26
Special interest groups, 76

T-U

Taylor, Paul, 13
Technology, 119

board of directors mindset about, 122, 123
budgeting for implementation, 129–130, 132–133, *see also* technology spend
dedicated resources, 124, 129
defined as, 121
delivery mechanisms, 124–125
listservers, 126–127
managing expectations of, 134–135
options matrix, 135–136
philosophies for the future, 126
planning to implement, 127–129
positions in association regarding, 129–130
questions to ask, 137–138
return on investment, 131–132
small-scale testing, 133–134
technology spend, 130–131
Texas Trial Lawyers Association (TTLA), 90–91, 141–142
DepoConnect, 141
TrialSmith®, 141–142
Townsend, CAE, Tommy, 141
Trade associations, 78
Trade shows, 19–20
Trends affecting association membership
career stage, 16–17
competition, 18–20
generational differences, 15–16
market structure
consolidation, 12–14
specialization, 14–15
technology, 20–22
time, 5–9
technological influence on, 6–7
value expectations, 9–12
TrialSmith®, 141–142, *see also* Texas Trial Lawyers Association
Truncale, Joe, 92–93
TTLA, *see* Texas Trial Lawyers Association

V
Volunteers
committees, 48, 51–52, 57–58
expectations, 9
"Just in Time" use, 53
training, 52
trends in, 57–58
Volunteer–staff relationship,
board self-evaluation, 70
performance appraisals, 70
planning cycles, 69–70
survey feedback, 70

W-Z
Web 2.0, 22
Wilcox, Pamela, 5, 51
William E. Smith Institute for Association Research, 17